THE RED TOY

By

Med Magill

***

Many thanks to dear friend Tyre Dupuy for her tireless editing of my original story.

Part I

When my master opens the car door, I hesitate. Normally I bound out and head to the nearest tree or bush. But today is different. We are not where we once called home anymore. For what seems to be the third time in as many years, my master has moved again.

I sniff the air, and it seems very hot and moist. South, we are much farther South, I can smell and feel it. "Come on Axel," I hear my master say. I look into her eyes and can tell it is safe. I leap down to the driveway where she has parked her SUV. The concrete feels hot under my feet. Wow, we must really be farther South. I quickly look and see a long driveway. That is unusual. Never been to a place like this. Off in the distance through the trees I see a bridge, a big one. I can also smell a river, even though we seem to be a good distance from it. From the other side of the yard, I can see a tall pointed building. It seems to stand off on its own. At the top, it looks like a glass enclosure, maybe a light. On the very top, there's a flag pole flying the American Flag.

"Come on Axel, come see your new yard," she says. I follow along beside my master. She opens a gate and there before me is what seems like a park. It's a huge yard with shade trees and luscious green grass. I rub against my master's smooth ankle and look up at her. "Go on," she says, and nods her head towards the park. I trot over to the nearest shade and take a look around. My master climbs up a short set of stairs just past the gate. From there, she plays with her keys, eventually going into the new, strange house. It seems to be mostly brick, much bigger than what we lived in up North.

So this will be our new dwelling until she moves again, it seems. Not bad. It's quite the improvement over the itty-bitty apartment in the city of humans called St. Louis. The grass feels wonderful under my paws. I nuzzle my head into the ground initially, but soon find myself rolling around in the grass. I did not smell the presence of another cat, so it was going to be just my yard.

I hear the screen door bang, and I look to see my master coming out, moving towards her SUV. She begins grabbing boxes and bags and moving them into our new house. I roll around and watch this. I think I'm happy about this move for a change. The last one from the little house to the closet, called an apartment, was not a good move for me. This is definitely a huge improvement.

"Come on Tommy, go get it, come on," I hear faintly from somewhere nearby. It sounded reasonably close. I perk my ears up and listen again.

After a moment I hear "Aw come on, Tommy, go get it." This time I can tell it's coming from the very back of our new yard. I scamper towards the back. Gosh, what a great yard we have now. I run at least 50 yards before I come upon woods. "Come on boy. No, don't roll over, go get the toy over there," I hear closer, it seems.

After another 30 or 40 yards of woods, I come upon a wooden fence some six feet high. No problem for me. I climb up one of the posts and sit. Beyond the fence are more woods, but I can see a clearing of grass much like my new yard? I quickly look back towards our house and see my master moving, walking back to the vehicle to get more stuff. I know I don't have long before she'll look for me or call for me. I need to hurry.

I climb down the other side of the fence and hurry towards the clearing. I hear the voice more clearly now. Hiding low and behind a bush, I see the owner of the voice.

It is a young man, maybe 18 or so. He is kneeling and waving something in his hand. "Come on Tommy, come get it!" he yells with a bit of annoyance. I follow his eyes across the yard. About 30 feet away is something really big, orange and furry lying on its back. I see paws, tail and then realize, "My gosh, it's a cat like me." It's like me, but much bigger. Bigger is a nice way to say it. It is the fattest cat I have ever seen. It is an orange short hair calico cat. I have similar markings, but I'm more of a gray with some sprinkles of orange -- a mutt of a cat I guess you might say.

The big cat seems to rock back and forth as if it is scratching its back. I then realize it is trying to turn itself over. It finally succeeds and rolls over onto its huge stomach. The cat seems to be enjoying himself. He looks blankly back at the young man. This is what the young man sees, but what I see is this sly old "dog" ignoring his master, acting the fool for him.

"Ok Tommy, that's enough for today," the boy said. But I'm going to teach you to fetch this toy if it's the last thing I do."   He tosses the toy towards the fat cat as he stands up. The red colored toy rolls up and over the cat. He doesn't flinch. The cat then rolls over on its back as if to give up too. The young man stands and looks at the cat with disdain, then smiles. He walks over and kneels down to rub the fat cat's belly. I stifle a laugh, when off in the distance I see HER.

"HER" is another cat sitting on the deck of the house watching the boy and his cat. She has the most beautiful smile I have ever seen. A grey and white mix of long hair was her coat. I guess her to be two or three years old. I am simply stunned at her beauty. The young man trots up the stairs of the deck, and as he opens the door to go inside, he says to her "Hey, Julie, your buddy is one stubborn cat."

I am shocked out of my trance when I hear my master yell "Axel, where are you Axel?" I didn't want to go. I look back towards the fence and know I have to go, but first, I look back at the beautiful cat again and see her staring right at me. "Can she see me"? I wondered. I don't think so. I am well hidden behind a bush and tree. My master calls my name again. I have to go. The "beauty" steps down off the deck and begins walking towards where I am hiding. No! I jump back and scamper back to the fence and quickly jump on top of it. I take one last look and see she is watching me. Her eyes say "Hi." Oh my! I almost fall over the fence. I manage to land on my feet and quickly run back towards our house.

"Oh, there you are, Axel. Come on boy. Let's get you something to eat," my master says, walking towards the house. Inside, I feast on a can of Meow Mix. I then take a quick tour of the house. It's quite large for our standards, but probably a modest size for most humans. I see only one bathroom and two bedrooms. The meal makes me sleepy, so I curl up in the corner of what is probably going to be the den of our new home. As I close my eyes, I see the image of that beauty across the fence.

3

The next day I can't wait for my dear master to wake up. I want to go outside and explore. I want to see my new neighbors. In particular, I want to see that beauty again. In all my years of life, almost four years now, I always thought the prettiest cat was the Siamese cat. I'm embarrassed to say, I often fantasize about having a Siamese cat girlfriend. I think I may have a new favorite and her name might be Julie.

The sun is up at least two hours now, and my master is still asleep. I know she stayed up late into the night unpacking everything. A glance around the room, and I'm amazed how settled in it appears we already are. The boxes of clothes and kitchen supplies she loaded in from the vehicle are gone. She has put everything away.

I gently jump on the bed and begin to walk around her. At first, I stay a good foot away as I walk along her back to the pillow, then back to her feet. I move closer in and gently brush up against her back. I turn on the purring. Surely that will wake her; still, I get nothing. I think of jumping on top of her, but think better of it. She needs her rest.

I spend most of the morning exploring every nook and cranny of our new house. I find a neat fresh litter box in a small closet in what looks like a wash room. I take care of my business and check on her again. Nope, she is still softly snoring away. Poor master is so exhausted. I walk towards the back of the house and leap up on one of the window sills overlooking the backyard. It is a beautiful sunny day. I'm thinking about how I can't wait to get outside when I see her in the distance.

There at the back of the yard, I see that same beautiful cat from yesterday. It is Julie, sitting just at the edge of the woods staring at me. When she realizes I see her, she stands up and begins walking in a figure eight back and forth, all the while looking at me. The morning sun shines on her showing her beautiful fur. I look back towards the bedroom hoping my master is waking up, but I know she isn't. I get up the courage, and I raise my right paw and wave at this beautiful friendly cat. She stops and smiles. She nods her head, asking me to come over. I nod back telling her I can't right now. Through our minds, I tell her I'm stuck inside at least for now. She nods her head acknowledging it, and then she turns to leave. A glance back tells me to come on over whenever I can.

She disappears into the woods. For the first time since I can remember, I fail to land on my feet. When Julie disappeared from view, I leaned back to stretch and found myself falling backwards. With a loud thump, I landed flat on my back on, thank goodness, the carpet. "Ouch, that's smart," I thought to myself. A moment later, I feel myself being lifted into the air.

"Oh baby! Are you okay?" my master says as she picks me up and pulls me to her face. She nuzzles her nose into my side. I always loved that. I nestle my body against her and meow my gratitude. She places me down on the back of the couch and disappears towards the bathroom. I look out the window and can see that Julie is gone.

4

As with our other homes or apartments, my master likes to keep me inside most of the time. This new place, I hope, will be different. I want to get outside and see my new friends. My master sits down on the couch and turns on the TV. I nuzzle up against her several times trying to get her attention. When I do, I move towards the back door, hoping she gets the hint. It seems like forever, but she finally gets up and lets me out.

"You stay nearby, now Axel," she said as I scamper out. When I know she's not watching me anymore, I quickly run toward the back of the yard. I climb over the fence and then slowly start walking to Julie's house. On the deck I see Julie lying across one of the railings, sunning herself. Again, I am stunned by her beauty. I wonder how I should approach her. Should I call her or just walk up? Where is that Tommy cat? Not sure he would appreciate me at the moment. If I were him, I'd certainly be in some kind of protective mode.

Then, there are also the masters to keep in mind. They may not like strays around their cats.

When I look at her again, she's looking at me. Her eyes wink and tell me to come on up. I can't recall, in all my four years, ever being as nervous as I am right now. I walk slowly across the yard and up on the deck. All the while, I look, listen, and smell for the masters or the Tommy cat. As I get closer, Julie says "Don't worry, our humans love cats. They don't care about a stranger being around as long as it's a friendly stranger. Are you a friendly stranger, Axel?"

She knows my name! Her voice is mesmerizing. It is the softest, gentlest voice I have ever heard. "Yes," I said in a not-so-confident voice. I clear my throat, and as I walk up the steps of the deck, I say, "That sounds fine to me...uh...my name is Axel."

She smiles back and says "I figured that was your name when I heard your master calling for you." Of course, I said to myself, she would have known my name from that.

I feel a little bit embarrassed about that when, from behind me I hear, "Hi, my name is Tommy."

I find myself sitting on top of the railing trying to catch my breath. That huge orange cat Tommy scared the dickens out of me. I didn't know he was behind me and that close. When I catch my breath I say, "Hi Tommy, my name is Axel."

"Sorry about scaring you like that. Didn't mean too," he said to me.

"Oh, you didn't scare me" I blurt out. I look at Julie, and she is smiling at me. I then look at Tommy who is giving me a very surprised look. "Okay, you did startle me. I'm not used to someone sneaking up on me like that," I said to him. He gives me a hurt look and apologizes. I say, "No problem. I'm just a bit nervous around new friends." Boy was that ever true!

"Well I see you met my girl, Julie," he said glowingly and then walks over and nuzzles up to her. I look at him and then her. She is still smiling that dazzling smile.

"Yes, I did. My name is Axel. Darn it all, I said that already. I'm new, just moved here from St. Louis. I live right behind you guys."

Julie smiled and said so softly, "Well, Tommy and I are so glad to have a new neighbor, aren't we Tommy?"

Tommy looks at her and then to me, "Oh yeah, great to have a new buddy around here. The only other real buddy we have is old Plato, a few houses down from here. Well, then there's Spite and his buddies, but we don't want to go there."

"Plato"? I asked.

"Yes, Plato. He's sort of the old seer around here. Old, but very wise."

"We both love him dearly," Julie said.

"Well I would like to meet him too" I said. "What about this Spite and his crew"?

"Oh, you want to stay away from him. He's a stray that hangs out at the Winn Dixie, just round the block. He and his gang are no good. They come around here sometimes looking for food," Tommy quickly says.

"Okay, sounds like bad news. I will plan to avoid him," I said.

Julie, with those incredible eyes -- I have to really control myself and not give away the fact that I am really smitten by her. When I look at Tommy, I see he's truly smitten by her also. It is pretty apparent that Julie is Tommy's girl, and I will have to live with that. That thought saddens me and, unfortunately, Julie picks up on it. She seems to be a bit embarrassed by it all. I feel the urge to leave right then and try to think of a good reason to leave. Come on master, hoping to hear her from behind me.

Tommy then comes over and gives me a gentle bump with his massive body and says "Come on Axel, I'll show you around and take you over to meet Plato. You will love him." Then he somehow lowers his massive body down the steps of the deck. I look in fear that he would topple over, head first, but he doesn't.

I turn and look for Julie, but she has turned towards her house. She smiles and says, "You boys go on, have a good time. I'll see y'all when you get back." I look into her eyes and try to read what she is saying. She looks at me and seems to imply she is okay, to go on. I hop down on the grass and give a little bump back to my new friend. The gentle giant chuckled.

5

As we walk past three houses to this "Plato's" house, I find myself having to slow down and wait for Tommy. The guy can only move so fast. I measure him up as I walk beside him. He is at least four times bigger and heavier than I am. I have never seen such a giant of a cat.

"I know, I'm fat, ain't I" he chuckles as we walk.

"No! I'm mean no, I've just never seen one of us as big as you are," I quickly say.

"I know. Me either. Well it's not my fault; they feed me all this dry food that makes me this way".

"Well you are quite impressive is all I can say" as I bumped, or tried to bump up against him.

He laughs and then bumps me off my feet. He apologizes as I struggle back to my feet, and we both laugh.

Finally, we come upon an old plantation-style house, much bigger than the other human homes. It is badly in need of paint.

I asked, "This Plato lives here?"

"Yes and no. You see he lives under this house," Tommy said.

I soon find myself following Tommy through an opening at the base of the front porch of the house. There, under the porch, is an old cat, lying peacefully in the sunshine passing through several holes in the flooring above.

Without moving or looking, the cat says "Good morning, Tommy. Who is your new friend?"

"How did you know it was me, Plato, and how did you know Axel was with me?" Tommy asked.

"Well, first of all, I felt the ground moving as you came nearer 'Tank.' Secondly, I smelled your new friend, someone I hadn't smelled before. I bet his name is Axel, too."

I look at Tommy, and he has a look of amazement. He looks at me then mouths "How did he know that?" I guess the simple giant never realized he said my name when he answered the old cat's question.

"Oh, Plato, you are so smart. You need to teach me some of those things one day," Tommy said.

"Not smart, my dear Tank, just very experienced. You live and learn, and I have lived many a year now."

He rolls up slowly and then stares at me with very kind and very wise eyes. I have seen these same kind eyes somewhere else recently, but I can't place it just then. There is a loud clang of metal cans to my right, and I see that Tommy has accidently sideswiped a stack of empty cat food cans with his massive girth. "Dang it son, can't you be a bit more careful?" Plato said, not in a stern manner, but gently.

"Sorry pops," Tommy replied. Pops, I thought to myself. Of course, those eyes are the same as Tommy's, gentle, kind eyes. They must be kin.

"Y'all are related?" I asked. Plato looks at me. An eyebrow hitches up on his face. Oops, I think to myself, I haven't even introduced myself. "I'm sorry, Mr. Plato, my name is Axel. Just moved in behind Tommy and...and, "Julie," I say timidly. He looks at me with those kind eyes and seems to acknowledge my dilemma with Julie and Tommy. Can I be that easy to read? I need to be more careful or I may be ruffling the feathers of my new friend, Tommy, or worse yet, this Mr. Plato.

6

"Hmmm, I smell vittles, got to go!" Tommy says as he moves to go to his house. "You coming Axel"?

I look at him then back at Plato. I then tell Tommy, "I'll catch up with you, Tommy. I would like to talk with Mr. Plato a little bit more if he doesn't mind."

Tommy looks at me, then to Plato, who shrugs his shoulders as if to say, "fine with me". He then moves his huge bulk out into the yard to begin his journey home.

After a few nervous moments of silence, Plato says softly, "She is a beauty alright, my friend. Beautiful outside AND even more beautiful on the inside."

"Who is that?" I feigned ignorance. Plato laughs as he stands and arches his back in a long stretch.

"You know who," he says smiling at me. He then starts to walk out from under the porch. As he steps into the yard, he says "Come on my new young friend, Axel. I smell the food my masters have left out for me. He moves on without looking back. I follow him.

At the back of the massive house, there is, indeed, a small plate with what looks like the contents of some cheap cat food. The so-called "meat" had a smell of no animal I knew. Plato laughs at the confused look on my face.

"It's not that bad, really. You can half it with me. I rarely need more than a few bites in the morning," he says to me.

I watch him eat three or four bites, then step away, nodding for me to help myself. I'm really not hungry, but I do not want to insult my new friend by refusing to eat something that is good enough for him. I move closer and take a sniff. That is the problem, I needed to "not" sniff, just eat. Plato is right. It is really not that bad. I quickly realize that I have eaten the plate clean. I look apologetically at Plato, and he waves me off laughingly.

He then turns and walks towards the back of the yard without saying anything. I assume he wants me to follow, which I do. The yard of this house is in much disrepair, in need of mowing and weeding. Off to the right is an extremely old car with all the tires flat. I continue to follow Plato, walking all the way to the back fence of the yard. An evaluation of the fence indicates it is the same fence between Julie's and my home, just farther south. Plato then walks up a low hanging limb of a massive oak tree which leads eventually to the top of the fence. From there, he steps onto one of the posts.

I follow his lead and then sit atop the next post over. I see what appears to be the back of a large building. A concrete parking lot runs from the fence to this building. Around the side of the building I see several vehicles and humans going in and out of the vehicles to the building.

"A grocery store?" I said quietly to him.

"How very astute you are my new friend. Yes, a grocery store with name of Winn Dixie," Plato replies without looking away from the store. The name sounds familiar, Winn Dixie. Oh yes, that is the place that Tommy and Julie said this Spite character hung out.

At that, I hear a hiss. Then a cat comes barreling out of a trash bin. The solid black cat comes running right at us. Right behind it, three other cats spring out of the bin, chasing the black cat. A fourth cat leaps out of the bin and it watches the others cats chase the black one.

The look on the black cat's face is of pure fear. Poor thing is probably no more than a year old. Plato is calmly watching. The three cats chasing the black cat are menacing, and obviously feral, never touched by human love. Each has the look of murder in their eyes. I fear for the black cat. I feel the urge to do something. "Don't worry, he'll be alright," Plato said softly. I fight the urge to jump down and help.

When it appears the gang of feral cats are about to catch the black cat, he leaps through an opening of the fence below us. With that, the three other cats crash into the fence so hard that it almost sends me falling over on top of them. The three cats bellow a series of curses and slangs I had not heard in several years. Plato looks down on them smiling. I look back and can see the black cat scampering away. When I return my gaze to the mess below me, there is the fourth cat sitting closer. He has a mean ugly look. He looks in disdain at his partners in crime. He then looks up at me with a grimace, then to Plato. "You enjoying yourself Plato?" the leader says with a snarl looking at Plato.

"Oh yes, quite immensely. Seems your friends don't learn from mistakes too well. Didn't they do exactly this same thing yesterday?" Plato replied laughingly. The leader then hisses at his gang who quickly gather themselves to move behind him. He then focuses his gaze on me. A chill went up my back. He seems to chuckle at my reaction.

Without taking his eyes off of me he asks "And who's your friend here, Plato?" "Don't say my name", I'm thinking, when I hear Plato say,

"His name is Axel. He just moved in." I fight the urge to groan.

The leader's eyes narrow at this. He then stands up and begins a very slow and deliberate walk in the familiar figure eight pattern, all the while not taking his eyes off of me. The three behind him seem to take his cue and begin to stare daggers into me. The leader then says in a menacing tone, "I'm sure you've explained to this youngster the boundaries around here, right Plato? Like this building, this parking lot, this whole block is mine. No other cats allowed". The three cats behind the leader then in unison lower their heads and give their most sinister looks.

I admit being quite nervous at this point. I hope I'm hiding it, but I'm sure Plato can sense it. Does this gangster see it? Plato then says "I think you just explained it yourself, Spite."

Oh, so THIS is the Spite that my new friends said to avoid.

"The name is 'Spike' old man. 'Spike' not 'Spite.'" the leader says angrily back at him.

Plato smiled, "I like Spite. Seems to fit better". Spite begins to fume even more at this.

"One day old man--you better not ever lose your grip on that high perch. You slip and fall on this side of the fence, and me and my friends are going to love tearing your old rancid fur to bits."

At this, I puff up and say before realizing, "Hey there, there's no call to talk to him that way." I wondered to myself, "Did I just say that?" How I wish I could take it back!

Spite's menacing yellow eyes move their focus from Plato to me. A sneer forms on his mouth, showing rotten teeth, but gleaming fangs. He seems to be unconvinced of my statement. He raises a paw showing long, sharp claws. He points it at me. "You... Axel, is it? I am not talking to you, but since you feel the need to interject yourself into our conversation, what I said goes for you, too!"

I hear what seems to be Plato's claws digging deep into the post he is sitting on. Spite then runs and rams a shoulder into the fence below me, rattling it. Plato is ready for this I see then, but I'm not. I feel myself pitch forward. I am going over and down into Spite's three partners who are running towards the fence, greedily waiting for me to fall into their paws.

The only chance I have is to let go with my back paws and hope I can twist around and grab hold of the post with my front paws. I let go and pray as I twist as fast as I can and reach with my front paws. I feel my claws barely catch, dig them in, and pull hard. With much luck, they hold, and I pull myself atop the post. I am facing backwards. I squeeze my eyes hard, thanking heaven I didn't fall. I then open them and refocus. With as much patience as I could muster, I slowly turn around and calmly sit down in my original position and gaze down at them.

I can feel Plato laughing at them. Spite seems disgusted that his attempt to drop me down into his pack failed. He stands up. The three others back away, wary of what he might do next. He starts to walk back towards the Winn Dixie. He looks back as he walks away and says "You were lucky this time, Axel. Stay away and there won't be trouble, my friend." He turns his head and continues to walk away. His gang scampers along with him, keeping a safe distance from him.

I feel the urge to say something back at him, but I look at Plato, who smiles shaking his head back and forth, ever so slightly. "No," he was saying, "let it be."

He turns and lowers himself down onto the oak limb and walks to the ground. I watch Spite a moment more as they disappear around the corner of the building. I then climb down and run to catch up to Plato who is walking back towards his house.

7

"Well, that was interesting," I said, as I walk up alongside Plato. He says nothing and continues to walk. We go around the huge old house and back to his lair. There, Plato lies down in the same spot under the sun where I first met him. He looks at me with those eyes of wisdom for a long while then says "Axel, you seem to be a really nice cat. I want to warn you that, though I didn't seem bothered by our friend Spite, he is one bad apple. Stay away from him and his gang. Stay away from that area. That cat does not have one ounce of goodness in him. He will kill you for spite, hence my nickname for him. I've seen him do it before. He will do it again". He goes silent, then says, "You understand, son?" I feel closeness to this old cat that I have never experienced before.

I smile back at him and say, "Yes sir. Loud and clear." At this he seems to tire and lays down his head. This cat is a true friend.

He says without looking "That's good. Now you're welcome to hang around if you like, but this old cat is going to take a nap, okay?" I move closer to him. I want to buddy up to him. Instead I place a paw gently on one of his paws and say, "You rest, Plato. I'm going to head back. Sir, it is an honor to meet you. Hope to see you again soon." I turn to leave. As I exit from under the porch I hear him say "You're always welcome here Axel, anytime." I can hear him softly snoring away as I step out into the front yard.

I hustle back to my yard and make an appearance for my master. She is, as I thought she would be, beginning to look a little bit agitated and nervous, looking for me. I run up and rub against her legs. She coos, then picks me up in her arms and brings me inside. I really don't want to stay inside, but I really don't have a choice. After watching TV with her a little while, I squirm out of her hands before she falls asleep. Knowing this would awaken her, I run and rub up against the door, looking back at her. She sees that I want out and grudgingly gets up to let me out.

I sprint to the woods in the backyard. I can hear her yelling at me. I'm pretty sure she's saying something about not going too far. Too far is what I am worrying about. I cannot get Julie out of my mind, but I also know that Tommy loves her dearly. Neither has stated it directly, but it is obvious in Tommy's eyes. That cat loves Julie with all his heart. I am afraid I'm falling for her too, and she seems to like me also. Just what is going to become of all this, I don't know.

I bound over the fence and find the young man of the house again trying to teach Tommy to fetch. Over the following few weeks I learn the young man's name is Holden. I have to stifle my laughter because Tommy is rolling around on his back like a stuck turtle. "Come on Tommy, go get the toy" the young man says. He throws the red toy at Tommy. It actually bounces off his bulging stomach and comes to rest just a few inches away from him. Tommy is oblivious to it all. It seems he doesn't even notice that the toy has hit him. At that moment I catch Tommy's eye. He sees me sitting in the woods. I swear he smiles and winks at me. Then he rolls his massive body over to his stomach, lying directly over the red toy. The toy gives a weak squeak from under his enormous frame.

"There you go Tommy, get the toy, bring it here" young Holden yells to Tommy. Tommy acts as if he is listening to him this time, looking back and forth for the toy. "It's under you Tommy, right there," the boy points fanatically. Tommy looks in the direction the boy is pointing. "NO Tommy, there, under you!" the boy yells. Tommy stands up and runs off in the direction the boy is pointing, leaving the red flattened toy behind. The boy brings his hands to his face and groans. He walks over and picks up the toy and walks back towards the house. "Aw, forget it for now Tommy, but you're going to learn this one day, just wait and see," he grumbles as he walks up the deck.

As with yesterday, he stops by Julie sunning on the deck and gives her a nice neck rub. "Can't you put some sense into that boy, Julie?" he asks her. He then goes inside.

I run up to the deck as soon as the boy is gone. I ask, "Permission to come aboard, ma'am".

"Permission granted" she replied.

As I was about to take the first step I hear "Permission to come aboard...also". I leap all the way to the top of the deck from fright. Again, somehow, Tommy has snuck up right behind me. He says apologetically, "Aw Axel, I didn't mean to scare you again."

"How does he do that?" I wondered as I try to get my fur back to normal.

Julie is stifling a laugh as I stroll up. Tommy says something about taking a nap and starts walking over to a shady spot along the side fence of the yard. As I draw closer, I find I can hardly breathe because Julie is so beautiful. She smiles back at me which causes me to gasp. I feel myself starting to purr, and I can't stop it. She giggles at my purring. I try to act like it's nothing, but how do you hide that? Purring comes only when we are feeling affection towards something. Uncontrollably, I am exposing my affection for her.

"So what has you in such an excited mood Axel" she laughingly asks. I swear I am blushing red. My purring grows louder. I can't help myself. She stands up, arching her back. She strolls over to me and rubs against me, then circles around me. I can hardly think over the purring. I realize then that she is purring also. At that, she seems a bit embarrassed. We both find ourselves looking at Tommy who is now dozing. The purring stops. We both look at each other, and after a moment when realizing we had both stopped, we start laughing. I have now fallen in love with something else, her laugh.

I look back at Tommy, and though he is on his back and his head is upside down, he is watching me. This makes me feel very uncomfortable. I stand and move a few feet away from Julie and recline on my side. She notes my sudden change in mood. She glances over and looks at Tommy. She smiles at him, and then lays herself a few feet away from me. We both look at each other in silence for a few moments. She continues to smile, seeming to be so content. My smile starts to go away, thinking about how much I care for this beautiful cat that my new pal, Tommy, is obviously in love with. I must be some kind of friend, sitting here within sight of him and fawning over his girl.

Again, Julie seems to pick up on my mood. Its so hard to fool a fellow cat. We can read each other by our movements, our moods, our eyes. I watch her look over at Tommy for a long moment, and she smiles at him. This makes my heart sink. I try my best not to give myself away. Then, she smiles even broader at him. At this, I can't look at her. I look away. I try to think of something else.

Maybe I should pay Plato another visit, since his nap is probably over. He might be someone I can talk to about this. I turn to look at Julie, and she is staring intently at me. Trying very hard not let her beautiful eyes penetrate my feelings; I calmly and casually smile back at her. Her eyes soften, and then she says something I will never forget -- ever.

"I love Tommy," she says softly. My heart sinks, as I'm sure my shoulders do with that statement. She then says before I grow too despondent, "like a big brother." At this, I swear I get a crick in my neck, my head snaps up so fast. Looking into her eyes, I see she is telling me the truth. She does love him, but not as a partner in life, but as a sibling, a brother. Then she blushes. I blush too. After an awkward moment, I stand and move closer to her. I nervously move around to her backside, and then lay down next to her, pressing my side up against her back. We both start purring.

Off in the distance, I see Tommy stretch his legs. Then after a couple of rocks of his body, he rolls over on his side with his back to us. I nuzzle my nose into the back of Julie's neck. She stretches her head back towards me. I share a wonderful nap with her that afternoon.

9

The next three (or was it four) weeks go by fast. My master settles into her routine. She leaves for work well before sunlight and returns just before dark. The first week is tough because I can only visit my friends late in the evening and only for a few minutes. Tommy and I horse around a bit, and Julie and I cozy up and either nuzzle close together or stare intently at one another. These short times together mean so much to me. My heart aches for her during the day when I am locked up in the house.

Due to my arriving home late one night, thus worrying my master, I find her, on the weekend, working on the back door. She begins cutting a hole, and after she is through, I am delighted to see she has made a door to let me go in and out whenever I want. The thought of seeing my friends during the day is great, except for one thing. This new fangled doorway requires I wear a collar around my neck. The collar is not unattractive but I feel it slightly takes away some of my masculinity. I feel somewhat embarrassed walking around with it. The first time I go to visit Julie, Tommy howls with laughter at my new jewelry. "Oh, look at the handsome boy, Axel, with the pretty collar around his skinny neck," he said. Julie giggles with him. I can't help but laugh, too.

The next week I get to spend even more time with my friends. I make it part of my routine to visit with Plato at least once a day. I always look forward to his adventure stories. The more I grow to know him from our many conversations, the more evident his wisdom becomes. I asked him his age once, and he said he thinks he's seen 15 winters. Wow, I've never known anyone quite that old. He estimates he has 80 kids from a dozen or so litters in his lifetime.

During one of my visits with him, he senses something troubling me. Tommy has just left, leaving me alone with

Plato. He sees me watching Tommy amble away. Julie and I have grown very close, but I continue to harbor the feeling that I have taken her away from Tommy. I feel that he truly loves her more than he is letting on, but has just decided to accept the fact that she loves me as her boyfriend. This makes me sad for Tommy.

Plato picks up on my emotions. He says as I stare at Tommy, "He will be fine, Axel." I look at Plato and can see he knows my angst over this. "He's a big cat – a REALLY big cat," he says, making us both chuckle. "I mean, he is an adult cat. He will be fine. Your friendship, believe me Axel when I tell you this, means more than his dream of being more than a brother to Julie. Oh, he has always hoped for more, but he knows it's a dream only. He knows Julie loves him--but not like that. He hopes that this will change one day, but realistically he knows it won't. You haven't destroyed that possibility. You just eliminated that one-in-a-million chance. He loves you Tommy. In my eyes, you're the best thing to happen to him since Julie. He needs a friend like you. Julie needs a friend like you, too."

I look at him, his eyes so wise and intent. "I need them also, Plato. I also need a friend like you," I said to him, looking away before the tears begin. I never knew my father and never had a mentor type relationship before Plato.

He gets up, walks over and brushes up against me. "I know son. Too many of our youths never get to have an adult mentor. Not that I'm smart or anything, but I do try to be a friend to all young cats like you who will have me."

I leave that afternoon feeling much better about Tommy, about Julie. But there is still my nagging ache for Tommy. Would he have been better off without me coming into his life?

10

I begin to encourage Tommy to take walks with me around the neighborhood, trying to get him to exercise. During these walks I learn about Tommy's character. He loves Julie with all his heart, but he knows she doesn't relate to him in the same way she relates to me. Again, I feel badly for him. I have probably taken away any chance for him to be closer than a "brother" to her. He assures me again and again that he is very happy for her, that she deserves the best, and all he cares about is that she is happy. He feels she is very happy with me and, for him that is all that matters. I sense tremendous heartache in his voice when he says this, but he stills seems genuinely happy for us.

During one of our walks, I mention to Tommy how great it is to know Julie and him, how great it is to have him as my best friend and how much I truly care for Julie. Out of character, he looks at me with a stern face. He comes to a stop and looks away. I stop, circle around and face him. "You ok, buddy?" I ask.

He grimaces, and with his head turned away, he says "I'm truly very happy for both of you. It does my heart good to see my Julie so happy. And you, Axel, are a great friend." He pauses a moment, then he looks intently at me, "I'm pretty sure I know you, and know you would never do such a thing, but hear me now. If you ever hurt my Julie in any way, you will have to answer to me."

I look into his eyes and see he is truly serious. I admire him even more as a friend at this moment. I smile and say, "You will never have to worry about that, my friend". His look softens, and he returns to his normal, happy self. I pounce on top of him, then scamper away yelling "Besides, you can't catch me anyway."

He laughs and actually begins to trot towards me. "Don't you worry, I might not catch you at first, but when I do, I'll sit on you and crumple you like an old dried-up leaf."

"A leaf......, huh." I said. We both begin to laugh.

I now join Julie in the afternoons watching young master Holden, again and again, trying to teach Tommy to fetch. We laugh silently as Tommy always plays the dumb, a simple cat for the young man. Tommy isn't smart, but he isn't as dumb as he portrays for the boy. After five or ten minutes of tossing and chasing down the red toy himself, the boy gives up, as usual, and heads inside. I grow to be comfortable around the boy. He seems to like me, and gives me a pat or two when I am within reach. "Hey stranger, who do you belong to? I bet to that pretty new neighbor behind us" he says. Somehow, he has learned my name and always says "Hey Axel," from then on.

11

After several months, Julie and I try to meet a few times a week late into the night, usually at midnight. It seems that Julie's house now has one of those pet doors like mine, except that hers does not require her to wear this peculiar collar. She wears one, but it's a nice one that looks perfect on her. It seems she is the only cat who uses the pet door at her house. Tommy rarely uses it because he can't readily squeeze through it. "I really think he can fit through now if he wants too, but it is a very tight fit" she said. I believe this is due to my daily walks with Tommy, trimming up my big friend.

When Julie and I do get together, it is pure bliss to be truly alone. I love nuzzling up close to her, feeling her warmth, and not just hearing, but feeling her purr. I love Julie intensely, and she loves me.

One particular night, we agree to meet at our usual place. I wait and wait for her at the fence between our houses. She doesn't show up, which is so unlike her. I creep to the edge of her woods to look closely into her house and see nothing. Since the moon is nowhere in sight, it is very dark except for the street lights in front of the house. She is not going to show, it appears. I feel so lonely without her. I don't want to go home, so I decide to check on my old friend, Plato. When I get to his home and check under the porch, he is nowhere to be found. I think it very unusual because he is not the type to wander at night, especially this late.

I sniff around and smell that he has walked to the back of the house. Ah, to get a drink of water, I'm sure. I walk on back, but don't see him there. Something is wrong. The food that is usually half eaten is licked clean. The water bowl is empty and turned on its side. I sniff a bit and feel there is something new here. I unfortunately only realize what it is just before I hear someone say from the darkness behind me, "Well, well, look who's come to join us for supper." I stifle a yelp and slowly turn to see who I suspect it is. Spite's rotten teeth are showing through the darkness some ten feet away. The sound of snickering comes from both sides of me and behind me now. His three gangster boys are all around me.

Strangely, though, I am not afraid for me, I'm afraid for Plato. This fear seems to add a bit of backbone in me. If these gangsters have hurt my friend, I am ready and eager to fight them. Unconsciously, I grip the ground with my claws, ready to leap up or out in any direction if I need to. The odds are not good. I look at Spite. He moves a few feet closer, as do his friends. The sneer on Spite's face tells me there is no escaping this. I ask, "Where is Plato?"

Spite seems surprised at the question. "Plato he asks about. He better be more worried about himself than some mangy old cat, right fellows?" he says to his punks. They snicker at this.

I worry that something has happened to Plato. At that, I see Plato walk into the circle. He has been roughed up a bit. It seems I interrupted their party with him. This makes my blood boil. They had trapped poor Plato and were about to...., I shudder at the thought of it. I just happened along and ruined the party for them. I look at Plato, and he looks at me telling me he is fine. He looks at Spite and says, "Now, y'all have had your fun with me, so y'all move along now." Spite laughs, then the others laugh with him. I see Plato tighten his grip in the ground near me, getting ready to either pounce or run.

"Now, you listen here you mangy pieces of trash" Plato says sternly. I see he is not talking to Spite, but to the others. "I have never gone into your so-called "territory." Neither one of us has. You're on my territory now. You know that. You are in the wrong here. If you have any sense of decency, you can see that." I see the gangsters hesitate a bit, look at one another, then to Spite.

Plato looks at me and says with his eyes, the time is now. I hear him grip the ground tighter, his legs, though scrawny, are taut with muscle. I, too, tense and ready myself to follow his lead. I probably won't see the morning. I think of my Julie. I think of Tommy, and my master. But mostly I think of Plato. The first cat to go after him will be the first one I will sink my claws and teeth into.

From my left I hear a familiar voice, "Hey! Did I not get invited to the party?" The gangster cat to my left, moves out of the way and closer to Spite, revealing Tommy as he lumbers towards us. My heart leaps at the site of him. The odds are much better now. Though I don't think Tommy can fight, he can occupy at least two of them which leaves me and Plato with one each. I am hoping Tommy stands back and opens up the playing field a bit, but he walks right into the circle and stands next to me. The punk cat moves back to his spot, thus surrounding us again. With Tommy in our mix, I notice the gangsters have backed off a bit. Hmmm, do I sense a bit of fear?

Spite laughs and says "No, you're just in time my fat friend. We are just about to begin." This puts the fear back into me. I sense that Plato is tiring from his ready stance.

Tommy then says, in his usual slow drawl, "Well that's great. But I admit I'm a bit peeved you didn't invite me. Seems I have to invite myself to this "party," as you call it. What kind of games are we going to play?" Spite seems to sneer a bit more. We're about to play the game of life, I'm thinking. Then Tommy moves over to the gangster on the left. The gangster just stands there, surprised at the fat cat coming up to him. Tommy then does the most incredible thing. "Hey, maybe we can wrestle. You know how to wrestle, don't you? Come on boy," he says to him as he reaches a paw around the scrawny feral cat. With a humph, Tommy falls hard on top of the gangster. I swear I hear a bone or two snap. A stifled yelp comes from under Tommy.

Tommy rolls over and off the cat. As Tommy rocks back and forth to right himself, he says "Oops, hope I didn't hurt you there." The punk cat stands up and limps towards Spite feebly, whimpering and dragging one of its back paws. The gangster cat from behind me then runs over and leaps at Tommy head-on, digging his claws into him. Tommy laughs and calmly falls onto his stomach with the cat firmly attached. Again, I hear a stifled yelp. Tommy rolls over and off, and another gangster cat stands up slowly, it's back in an awkward position. "Aw man, I'm sorry, you surprised me there, hope you're okay". The gangster crawls to join his injured friend next to Spite.

Tommy rights himself and lumbers back, but this time he moves between Plato and the third gangster on the right. I can see that Tommy is bleeding from the claws that were dug into his fat belly. He doesn't seem worried about it. Tommy looks to the third cat and said, "Come on buddy, I'll try to be more careful this time." At this, the third gangster backs away and moves behind Spite. I look at Spite. To his left, I see two broken cats. To his right and behind him I see another cat filled with fear. Spite still has anger in his eyes, but he now sees three sets of eyes looking back at him. There is a long pause, and then Tommy says quietly, looking directly at Spite, "The party over?" Spite sneers, turns and walks away into the darkness. The gangster cats follow slowly behind.

When they are out of site, Plato says "Come on boys, let's go." We quickly move to the safety of the front of the house. There, Plato lovingly tends to Tommy's wounds. They are seriously deep cuts. He instructs Tommy to make sure his owners see them so they can take him to the animal hospital to get them looked at. There is a strong possibility of infection from the feral cats. Tommy, who is smiling the whole time up to that point, grimaces at the thought of going to the animal hospital.

We bid Plato good night and work our way back to Tommy and Julie's house. I ask him, "What are you doing out so late tonight? How in the world did you come upon us?"

I notice that Tommy is walking a bit slower, wincing a bit. The cuts seem to be taking their toll on him. Tommy says, "Well, Julie asked me to try and meet with you because she couldn't. Her masters accidentally closed her up in their bedroom for the night. She was frantic about missing your date, so she asked if I could go tell you what happened."

I think about that a while, then say, "We were supposed to meet close to two hours ago. I waited at our spot an hour before going to see Plato."

Tommy chuckles, and then says "I know. I sort of got stuck in that little bitty doorway for a while. I think the thought of squeezing through that door is hurting me more now than these little old scratches." He winces again. I move closer and sense he is really hurting. We are almost there.

"Okay, you know the plan, right? You're supposed to go inside and howl like you're hurting. They will get up and check on you and bring you to the animal hospital," I explain to him. He winces when I say animal hospital. Then he says "I know, I know. Don't remind me."

"Tommy, you were awesome, I said. You saved our lives, for sure."

He laughs and replies, "Aw, I don't know about that. I think you could have taken Spite by yourself."

I think to myself, yes, maybe I could have, but I definitely could not have handled him and three feral cats. Then there is our old friend, Plato. He would have suffered greatly, I'm afraid.

I practically lift Tommy's bottom to get him up the stairs of the deck. When we come upon the pet door, we both look at it, then at his stomach. There is no way he can go through it now. "These scratches are not going to make going through that contraption very fun," Tommy says. He was right. Worse, I feel it is going to be impossible. I suggest a slight change in plans; he starts the howling from the outside and then sticks his head through the cat door and meows away. He starts the poorest excuse of a howl I have ever heard. I back off and run back across the yard towards my house. I stop and look back and see the lights come on from inside the house. I can hear the masters talking to Tommy, as they fret over him and his wounds. Sure enough, 15 minutes or so later, their vehicle starts up and leaves for what I assume has to be the animal hospital.

My thoughts return to my poor Julie. I can't wait to see her tomorrow. Actually with it being so late, it will be later today. I want to tell her how much of a hero Tommy is.

13

That morning, after my master leaves for work, I hurry over to Julie's. No one is outside which worries me. I look down the driveway and see that the vehicle they left in last night is back. Daring to climb up on the deck to take a peek inside, I see Tommy, lying sprawled on the floor. His wounds, though still visible, are obviously cleaned up. His fur is shaved around his wounds, and they are painted pink. I chuckle and think how he probably hates knowing the color pink is painted all over his belly.

At first, I don't see her because she is almost completely hidden behind my huge buddy, but there's Julie, snoozing behind, but up close to Tommy. A lesser cat would be jealous, but I'm not. I know she cares for this gentle giant like a brother. I love him, too. I struggle about whether to meow to her or tap the window. I opt to head bump my head into the window. Julie's head pops up and she smiles at me. Her eyes look so tired and worried.

She rises slowly so as not to awaken him. She looks lovingly over at him, then moves around him and heads to the door. Her eyes tell me she will meet me at our spot. I quickly romp across the deck, down the stairs and towards the woods. It seems like hours before she comes, but I'm sure it is only a few minutes. She finally comes, and we exchange hugs and nuzzle for several minutes before either of us speaks. Before she can say a word, I say "Honey, don't worry about missing our date. Tommy told me what happened. Let me tell you what kind of hero our boy, Tommy, is. He saved my and Plato's life. If he hadn't shown up when he did, Spite and his gang would have had us." Whew," I say, after spewing that out as quick as I could.

She stares at me in silence. Then tears appear, and I hug her hard. "It's okay Julie; everything is okay. Tommy saved the day," I try to say to calm her. She cries into my shoulders for a long while.

She finally gathers herself, backs away and looks at me. "Last night was so horrible, Axel. I couldn't meet you for our date, and then Tommy gets hurt trying to deliver my message to you. I feel so guilty about it all," she says through tears.

I try to comfort her saying, "No, no, no. You have nothing to feel guilty about. Because of you, Tommy was there to help us. I'm telling you, I dread the thought of what could have happened if he hadn't been there." This seems to calm her down a bit. She then sits wide-eyed as I tell her the details of last night's adventure. When it is all said and done, we both agree that Tommy is a genuine hero.

14

Yes, Tommy is a true hero in my eyes and the best pal a cat can have. At this, that nagging guilt about him and Julie hit me. Julie senses something is up. She looks intently in my eyes to see what is wrong. I look long and hard into her mesmerizing eyes. I then look down, feeling like the worse heel there is. "What is wrong my dear Axel?" she asks me. I gather my thoughts and tell her what has been haunting me since we met.

"Tommy, it's our Tommy. He loves you so much, Julie," I said, and had to stop to control my tears. She looks at me, imploring me to go on. I continue. "Oh, Julie, I feel so bad for him. He loves you more than anything in the world, probably more than any cat can. I come along and take you away from him. I love you dearly, Julie, but it is not fair to Tommy. I truly feel if I hadn't come along, with time, Tommy and you could be together, not as brother and sister, but as a loving couple like we are now. I love you so much Julie, but I feel badly for my best friend, Tommy." At that I struggle not to breakdown like a little kitten.

She pulls my head up and stares into my eyes. Her eyes help calm me, as always. She then says something so beautiful to me. "Oh my dear, Axel, I do love him. But it is you I love as my soul mate. I know he loves me, and he will always be a part of my life, but all you and I can do is love him back. Still not feeling better, she says, "I love him, Axel, but my soul was empty until you came along." We then hug each other long and hard.

I check on Plato the following day to talk about our "party," and he seems to be back to his old ways, sunning peacefully. We discuss the "party" incident, and both agree that Tommy truly saved us from certain doom. Plato confides to me that he had plans to go right at Spite if a fight actually started. He knows he would not have survived the attack, but he was going to leave some scars on the thug. I shiver at the thought of seeing my old friend jumping on Spite, who after fending off a swing or two of Plato's claws, would have sunk his fangs deep into Plato's neck.

After a few days, the news of the "party" is known throughout the neighborhood. Neighboring cats come to give their thanks to Tommy for his heroic deed. How they learned about this is a mystery to me. I can only think that my old friend, Plato, may have mentioned it to a few felines. It makes sense. What better way to pump up your son's reputation? Sure enough, some single females come by to see our hero. Soon there are several of them swooning over the gentle giant with the pretty pink scars on his belly. Julie and I watch this with some humor over the following days. The boy is going to be okay, I think. He will eventually meet a new love. Ironically, one of the young beauties doting over Tommy is a Siamese. I laugh. That is his revenge against me. Best of all, news comes that Spite had not been seen since the "party." Good riddance, I thought.

The following weeks turn into months. Life is good. Julie and I spend as much time as possible together. Sometimes we enjoy the company of Tommy and one of his handful of girlfriends.

Such is life, and just when I think life can't be any better, it all comes crashing down.

Part II

The first inkling of possible trouble in my life is when my master comes home one day with a package of some 20 flat pieces of cardboard. I have seen this several times before--moving boxes. They sit against the wall for several weeks, so I begin to think it is nothing. But one morning, instead of running off to work, my master stays and starts packing.

Oh, no, I think. We are moving again. My mind races with fear of losing my Julie, of losing my best friends, Tommy and Plato. While pacing back and forth outside, I fret over how to break the news to Julie. This will surely upset her. I don't want her to suffer such pain. My mind races on my options. The only option I can come up with is to run away and hide. It will hurt to lose my master, who has been so good to me, but I have to choose between her and my Julie. My master will search long and hard for me and suffer greatly at my loss, I'm sure. Eventually, though, she will accept that I am gone and move away with the big trucks.

That is the way I plan to explain it to Julie - after the fact. If I tell her of my plan now, I know it will worry her to know to death that I'm moving, so it's better not to let her know. When the big trucks come to pick up the moving boxes, I will run away then. Only after my master has given up hope and left will I let Julie know what almost happened. But is it the best plan, I think to myself. I must talk to Plato and get his input.

I run over to see him. Along the way, Julie sees me and calls me to come over. I can't just wave and continue on or she will know something is up. I decide to stop and talk with her. My heart aches at the sight of her, thinking of the prospect of moving away. We hug and she asks where I am headed. I hesitate a bit then calmly say, "Oh there's something I want to ask Plato."

"Ask him what?" she asks.

"None of your business," I said laughingly while searching for a good reason.

"What?" she says sternly to me, a gleam in her eye.

"Just kidding" I say, and then it hits me. "Uh, I just want to ask him if he has seen Spite around. He would know. I hear there are some sightings of him."

"Really? Hmmm, seems I would have heard that, too," she says, sensing the lack of truth in my statement. I hate fibbing to her. She smiles and says, "Go ahead, I'll see you later darling."

I start to turn the corner when I hear her say, "I'll give you this one, Axel. Don't fib to me again, okay?"

I wince at that and reply, "Sure thing, honey" then quickly run to Plato's.

2

When I get to Plato's, I find him resting on a limb of one of the massive oak trees on the property. I jump up on the branch and settle down a few feet away from him and don't say anything. As usual, Plato doesn't give away that he's even noticed me. I look at my dear friend, and my heart sinks at the thought of moving away.

"What's bothering you, Axel? It can't be that bad," he says without even looking at me. I lower my head down to the limb, trying not to start crying like a kitten. He senses my pain. He gets up and moves closer to sit next to me. "What is it, son?" he asks me softly.

I gather my thoughts then blurt out, "Plato, its bad news. My master is starting to pack again. I know we will be moving to a new place, and I'm sure it's very far from here." I drop my head down and can't speak anymore. He moves closer to me and places a paw on my head. He seems at a loss for words. After a long moment, he asks, "And so your plan is?"

This clears my head a bit. I do have a plan, a good one too. I smile at him and say "You always know what to say, wise man." He smiles a weary smile back at me. I then tell him of my plan to run away when the big trucks come. He thinks it's a good plan. He even offers for me to hide out with him until the trucks leave. Then he says, "So what is it you've really come to see me about. You seem to have the plan pretty well thought out. What perplexes you, my friend?"

It is Julie, of course, whether to tell her my plan or not. I say, "I don't know if I should tell Julie. I know she will fret about it until my master is really gone. I'm leaning towards not telling her until it's all over and done."

He seems to think about it for quite some time before answering me. He looks at me and says, "I think you are right, Axel. For example, what if our Tommy suddenly becomes ill and his owners have to rush him to the animal hospital. He is gone all day, but then he comes home all healthy and fine. For the whole day, we would all be upset wondering how sick he is, if there is something seriously wrong with him and if he's going to come home. On the other hand, if we see him only when he's back, all fine and dandy, then and only then we are told of his close call, that would have saved us a day of worry. Which way would you rather hear the news?

I laugh at his very familiar story and, of course, say I would rather hear the near death experience after, than before. I leave him feeling much better, but I still don't feel better about trying to act as if nothing is wrong around Julie during this time. I will bide my time, waiting for the big trucks to show so I can then run and hide, all the while, acting as if nothing is wrong in front of Julie. It will be tough, but that's the way it has to be.

I then go see my Julie. She and I decide to lie around and nap for the rest of the afternoon. Little do I know it is the last time I will see her for almost a year.

3

That night, my master picks me up and takes me for a ride in her SUV. This is not unusual. She often takes me along for short rides when she is running errands. A lot of nights she takes me along to the Sonic where she gets a milkshake and shares a few spoonful's with me. This night I think nothing of it, but then we pass the Sonic. Okay, we're going to another place, I thought, no big deal. Soon we are on the big highway, and by the look of the stars that night, we are heading north.

I try to calm myself, thinking she is just going somewhere else. We will be turning back shortly. I climb into the back seat and lie down to try to sleep. I figure if I go to sleep, I will wake up at home after she gets to where she is going and turns around. I shiver as I look behind the seat to the storage area. Normally it is clear. The thought of seeing luggage there frightens me. I brace myself, stand up and peer over the back seat. There, before me, are luggage bags along with a couple of the moving boxes.

I sink down in the seat and close my eyes. We are heading north, away, for good. What about the big trucks, I thought? I hadn't seen them. I can only guess they are picking up the rest of her belongings later. We are not going back. My heart aches at the thought of not ever seeing my friends again, worse, not seeing Julie again. Then I fall into more despair when I think of my Julie not knowing what has happened, only knowing that I am gone without even saying goodbye. Agonizing over this turn of events, I eventually fall asleep.

4

The sunlight comes through the windshield and wakes me up. I rub my eyes and peer outside. We are still on the big highway. My master sees me and utters something to me, something that sounds like going back home? It sounds like she says St Louis. The thought of moving back to that "closet" again pains me.

Around noon, I see a familiar sight, the great big arch, the one in St Louis. My heart sinks at seeing it. "We're almost home, Axel," I heard my master say. Soon we are going in circles in some kind of parking garage. We park, she picks me up then we go into the small room that moved us up. The doors open, and we walk down a narrow hallway that reminds me of the little apartment we use to live in. She comes to a door and starts putting a key in it, "We're here!"

The door opens up and the room is filled with sunshine. She drops me to the ground, and I quickly go to look out a window. This is not the old closet we use to live in. It is much bigger, but smaller than the house we just moved from. I look out the window, and I can see the big arch, but it is below us. Behind the arch, I see the big river, the same one I somehow know we just moved away from, but much farther north. I lay down, despondent over it all. I think about Julie, Tommy and Plato. I feel so sad.

My master makes several trips back and forth, bringing in her luggage and boxes. The apartment is furnished with the human furniture. I see there is only one bedroom and one bath. My new litter box is placed in a small closet space in the small kitchen. Eventually she opens a large window that leads out onto a patio. From here, I look down and see we are very high in the air. I have never been this high before. This is my new "home."

5

The days drag by slowly. The big trucks must have gone to the old house and picked up the boxes because they appear in the new place a couple of days later. Soon, everything is unpacked and put away. My master leaves early and returns late as before, but this time, I am stuck in this small apartment all day. One evening she takes me for a drive. I so hope we are heading south and home, but we go to a Sonic and share a milkshake. I love my master dearly, but I miss my friends more. I feel they are gone forever.

The days turn to weeks. The weather gets cooler. I find myself constantly thinking about my Julie, but less and less about Tommy and Plato. It seems Julie's face is forever imprinted on my brain, but the others are becoming distant memories. I know this is the survival mode that is part of a cat's brain. It exists to help us live and adapt to our ever-changing environments.

That's why it's amazing that, somehow, Julie's memory has never gone away. I still ache for her presence and feel the pain she must surely be going through missing me.

Weeks turn into months. I turn four, but start to feel much older. I feel so empty inside. I adjust to my new surroundings, eventually, because I have to. New toys are given to me, and I play with them. I snuggle closer to my master when we sleep together, but when I close my eyes, I see Julie and dream about being with her.

6

Then, one night a strange thing happens. My master comes home and lugs in a packet of the large cardboard pieces that turn into boxes. I am very confused at this. It is maybe four or five months, at the most, since we moved here. Why does she have those, I thought? It is too early to be moving again.

She begins packing. Humming to herself, she seems happy about it. I move close and rub up against her. She smiles at me and says "That's right, we're moving again." At this, I sag to the ground. Not again, I thought. Where, I wondered. She says something about snow. Further north is the only thing she can be talking about. Further away from Julie is all I can think about.

No. Not this time. I just can't move again. I hunker down and start planning my escape. I know I have to act fast. I cannot be caught off guard again. I know it will be hard on my master, but she is human, and I am only a cat. She will get over it. I have to escape before the move north. It is too far away and, unlike from here, I won't be able to find my way back south. I know that big muddy river I see every day flows within miles of where Julie lives. If I follow that river, I will eventually get there; that is, if I survive.

I spend every waking moment devising my plan. It requires quickness on my part, and I've gained at least a pound or two being locked up in this little apartment. I figure, though, I'll use those extra pounds to live on when I'm starving my way back south. I start practicing leaping, pouncing, jumping from one piece of furniture to another. My master thinks I've gone crazy, but she laughs each time she sees me. I need to get stronger.

7

After a few days, it seems there is nothing left but boxes and furniture in the apartment. Moving day must be close. I realize my escape relies on my master because going off the balcony is not an option. I cannot climb down this slick building. It is not a tree. I can't dart out into the hallway. That doesn't lead me down. The little room can, but I can't make that happen by myself. No, I need her to take me for another ride.

At night, the time comes. She picks me up and takes me down in the little room. As the time comes closer, I look into my master's kind eyes. I dread the pain I am about to bring to her, but I have no choice. She is a strong woman, and I know she will be fine, eventually, but it doesn't make it any easier to accept what I have to do.

We step out into the cool air. I smell the river just a few blocks away. I look and see that from here I can make my way down eventually to ground level to the street. It is time. I lick her hand to say good-bye. She smiles down at me. I start to try and squirm out of her hands. Her grip tightens. I sense her fear of me getting out of her clasp. I squirm again and realize for her to loosen her grip, I will have to put the dreaded plan two into action.

I close my eyes to get courage. I yowl loudly and dig my claws into her arms. It hurt me as much as it did her, I'm sure. She yelps, and her grip loosens. I squirm out and fall to the ground with a hard thud, but on my feet. I run under the nearest vehicle. I hear her scream my name. I run from under one vehicle to another, then another. Her screams grow fainter. I can hear the fear in her voice, but I steel myself to keep running. I see an opening to another level below and jump down to a nearby vehicle, then down to another level and another and eventually onto the ground outside. The feel of the grass feels strange to me. I try to remember the last time I felt the grass like this. It was the last time I saw my Julie. I run across a street after checking to make sure there are no vehicles. I run under a truck and stop to catch my breath.

I can hear my master in the distance frantically calling for me. I fight the urge to head back to the safety of her arms, the arms that are surely badly scratched by me. I wince at the thought of it. I know I have to get farther away, farther so I can't hear her anymore.

I run from one dark spot to another. Cars and trucks whizz by me on the street. My heart is pounding. I am scared to death of being crushed by one of them. I sniff and smell that the river is closer. I run and run and eventually make it over the levee and to the river. I sit and shiver against the cool air. The timing of my escape couldn't be at a worse time. It is winter and will be cold for several months more. I can see a tugboat pushing several of the flat boats down the river. I wonder if it is possible to hitch a ride on one of them all the way back to Julie.

8

Knowing I will have to do most of my traveling at night, I continue moving south along the river and the levee. After a while, I seem to be on the outskirts of the city. The sun is coming up, and I think about my master. How sad she must be. I feel badly for her. I miss her, too, but I know I have to get back to Julie somehow. This is just how it has to be.

When the sun is up, I realize how tired I am, and cold. I come upon an area of buildings that project out onto the river. There are boats tied up to the pier. I find a pile of rags that smell of gas and decide that this is not the place to be. I walk up to the top of the levee and see a small stand of trees not far off across the road that runs along the levee. I work my way there and try to sleep. I do sleep, but fitfully. I keep thinking of Julie and how sad she must be. I keep hearing my master calling frantically for me. Have I done the right thing? Life was good with my master; she was kind to me and loved me dearly, I know. But Julie needs me, and I have to get back to her, even if it means I have to die trying.

There are all kinds of sounds around me, mostly of cars and trucks passing by on the levee road. I guess it must be close to noon when I decide to move on. I am hungry and thirsty. Water is easy to find, I know, but what about food? I work my way back to the levee, up and over and down to the river. I taste the water, and it tastes unclean, but I have no choice. I walk around the group of buildings I saw earlier and continue down river. I am seeing lots of rats on my journey so far. Though I have never eaten one, I know I will probably have to eat them to survive.

I ignore them along my walk, but do keep tabs on how close I can get. I figure when the time comes, it will be best to put them between the river and me. Then I can close in on them and try to make it a quick killing. I dread the thought of it.

I eventually come upon what looks like a place a few humans have gathered recently, a picnic spot maybe. I sniff through several beer bottles and papers strewn all around. I find a half-eaten hamburger and devour it. It's not too tasty; I hate ketchup, but it does the trick.

The days drag on. I travel mostly at night and sleep during the day, always moving south with the river. Along the way, I see many interesting things. I see a huge fish lying on the side of the river bank, having been dead a long time. It has a long skinny snout with many pointed teeth. I think of eating some of it, but the stench is too much. I keep expecting to come upon snakes along the way, but realize it is winter, and they are burrowed in deep for the winter. Lucky me! The weather is not too cold, at least no snow yet. The worst is the rain. When it comes, I seldom can find shelter from it. I get wet and shiver with the coldness, but keep moving.

One evening a family appears at the top of the levee. It looks to be a mother and father with three little ones. They spot me. The parents warn them to stay away, but one of the kids throws a candy bar down to me. I run to it, grab it and move away. I eat it, but I have to admit, it isn't sitting on my stomach very well, but you do what you have to do.

Dogs are a definite problem. Fortunately, they are not very good at sneaking up on you. I can smell them well before they can see or smell me. When I sense them around, I look for the nearest tree or high perch. One night a pack of four dogs sees me up in a tree and barks and hounds me all night. I feel safe up high, but I begin to worry they might not ever leave, but when daylight appears, they finally run off.

My fellow cats are my worst fear. They can sneak up on me if they so desire. Most of the time, I see them or sense them and stay well clear of their territory. I'm sure most are friendly, but some are not, and I can't afford an injury that could slow me down. One did manage to see me without my being aware of it. Fortunately for me, it was a friendly old cat. He sensed my quest, it seems, and said good luck to me with his eyes.

9

Unfortunately for me, this muddy Mississippi River has so many bends in it. I find it frustrating that, while following the river, I can be travelling west, then east, then even north sometimes, all the while heading south. I then realize it can save me a lot of time if I travel directly instead of following the river, so I weigh my options and decide to go for it. It involves crossing fields of high grass and avoiding cattle everywhere.

One day, as I'm crossing a field, I hear a voice calling out to me "Hey!" I jump straight up and when I land, I look back to see a black cat lying in the grass watching me. "I haven't seen you around here before. Sorry to startle you, boy," he says with a soft friendly voice.

I say, "No problem, sir. I'm just trying to follow the river, just passing through."

He looks at me curiously. "The river? That's a long ways from here that way. It's just behind me, over there," he says.

"Yeah I know. I'm working my way south. Thought I could take a short cut. I hope I'm not offending you by doing that," I say.

He stands up, and I see he is a very big cat, much bigger than me, but smaller than Tommy's size. He only has three legs. His front right paw is missing. He sees me staring at his missing leg and says "I know, looks goofy, huh? One of them dang cows crushed it accidently, and it had to be cut off. I feel lucky to be alive, though. Most other owners would have just put me down, you know?" Yes, I know I thought.

That is the thinking among the country folks. Being put down is always a lingering fear for us cats, especially country cats.

"You seem to manage quite fine with the other three," I try to say cheeringly.

"Yep, sure do. So my name is Lucky, what's yours?" he asked. Lucky, I thought. He seems anything but lucky to me.

"I'm Axel. I'm trying to get way down the river back to where I use to live to be with my soul mate, Julie."

"Soul mate? Lucky you. I haven't found mine yet. Kind of tough competing against you quads," he says with a laugh. I laugh with him.

Lucky starts hopping towards a large barn in the distance. "Come on sonny, I'm sure you're starved." I am, and follow along. After he acknowledges with his eyes that I have his permission, I feast on some dry cat food that is set out for him. The sun is going down, and I know I had better get moving. I am tired though and lonely.

He senses I am not excited about moving on. "Axel, you need to rest a bit before continuing on. Take a couple of days off, rest and bulk up. I have plenty of food," he says. The offer sounds so tempting. But I don't want to delay seeing my Julie for even one more day.

I look in the direction of the muddy river where I need to go. He follows my gaze and knows I am getting ready to leave. He then points to the northern sky. "You see those clouds there? Notice how they look little bit darker than normal?" I look and see what seems like pending rain. He smiles at me then says, "That's not rain, my friend. That is snow coming and lots of it, I'm afraid. You're better off waiting it out here for a few days. You can keep warm until it all passes."

Snow, I thought. The image of trekking through the snow along the river bank sends a shiver up my spine. Lucky is right. It is better to wait it out. I look at him for a long time. I then say, "Are you sure I won't be putting you out or anything by hanging out here. Your owners won't mind?"

He hops over and brushes against me and says, "No, and they won't mind either," pointing up towards the top of the barn. I look up and am shocked to see at least three other cats seated watching me, three old and weathered cats, it seems. One looks to be missing an eye. He speaks up for the three, "Cat, you best listen to Lucky mah fren, if you don't wants to be caught in dat snow when it comes down." Strange accent, I thought, and then recognize it immediately.

10

Lucky says, "So, you've been traveling for some time now? Well, my friend, considering your travels along the river, I'm surprised you're still alive. You didn't see me in the field or my buddies up there," he says half-jokingly.

He is right. I have been lucky so far. It is going to take a whole lot of luck to make it back to Julie. Is it impossible, I begin to think? Am I on a journey that can't be done? It's been two weeks, and I estimate I'm maybe a tenth of the way there, if that.

I look to him and nod agreeing with his assessment. I have been lucky so far. He senses my sadness and says "Every journey requires luck, my friend. Maybe over the next few days here, we can give you some tips. My friends up there have come from many places, some farther than where you are going. In fact, Tib up there is all the way from Cajun land in Louisiana." I look up at them, and they smile and wave. My new friend is right. I need to hole up for a few days and let the weather pass. Maybe I can learn from these guys, especially the Cajun cat called Tib.

The snow comes just as Lucky said it would, but even
he didn't think it would be this bad. It snows for four straight
days. The snow piles are higher than I can see over. On the
fifth day, the sun comes out with clear skies. No snow finally,
but then comes the bitter cold. That lasts another three days.
A week is now gone, and no progress towards my Julie. I do
spend lots of time with Lucky and his crew of old cronies.
Each one has a unique story. Each gives me helpful advice for
my journey.

11

As promised by my new friends, much of our
discussions are centered on my best options for getting back
to my Julie. I do not know the name of the town she lives in,
but I describe how I can see a bridge across the muddy river
to the north and south of me. I mention the tall building I can
see that comes to a point and has a light that shines down
from it at night. The one-eyed cat, Tib, thinks that I might be
talking about Baton Rouge. That name does sound familiar I
say. "Yes, mah fren, I tink you be talkin bout de Red Stick,"
he says in his Cajun dialect. He sees the confusion on my
face when he says "red stick." "Dats watt Baton Rouge

means in de French, you know. I live dare not dat long ago." I now realize why I initially recognized his accent when meeting him.

When discussing time frames, it appears that he was living down there around the same time I was living behind Julie. He adds that is where he lost his eye. It seems he had a run in with a gang of cats, the leader a ruthless old cus who took his eye. He adds "I vowed I would never leave dat place till I got my vengeance. Well it came bout two years later. Low and behold, dat leader came to de river one night. I spied him and waited for him. I had him trapped. I jumped him and had him pinned down. He saw me and recognized me. He knew he wuz a goner and seemed to give up. Well my friends, I couldn't go through wid it. I let him free." As I listen, I want to ask so many questions, especially a better description of this bad cat that sounds so familiar to me. Sure sounds like Spite. But then Spite would not have given up, I thought. I let Tib continue.

"Dis cat seemed grateful. I wondered if I had made a mistake and jumped de wrong cat. I wuz bout to apologize when he says he wuz sorry for blinding my eye. I was taken by surprise by dis, too. As he walked away, I sez to him dat it's never too late to start over, mah fren. He tanked me, and I never saw him agin. By de next week, I wuz on a tugboat headin nort." Tib sat back, then smiled. "Dat is your ticket, my friend." I, as well as the other cats, look at him a bit confused. He looks at me, then at the others. He smiles and says, "De boat. Dat's how our fren can get back home."

12

Tib went on to describe how the boat he caught a ride on travels up and down the river all the time and that the captain of the tugboat is cat friendly. He likes letting strays come aboard and travel with him. When he comes to a port, some cats leave, some stay. That is how Tib got to the town of Memphis, south of here. After some months of wandering, he came across this crew and has been here ever since.

A tugboat, I thought. Yes, that would save me months of time. I ask Tib how long he thinks it would take me to get to Julie if I just keep travelling down the river on my own. He rubs his paw against his head and thinks about it. Finally he says "Oh, I would say bout two and half years, naw, make it tree years."

"Three years!" I yelp. No, no I thought, that was way too long. He sees my incredulous look. He adds "Even de tugboat took two weeks itself." I fall backwards onto the snow. Oh my, I was thinking this journey would take me a month at most. How wrong I was.

After the shock of it all, we spend the next few days planning how I am to find this particular tugboat and hitch a ride. Seems this boat is 13 or 14 bends of the river south of here. I am to come to a large city, the city of Memphis. After getting past all the bridges there, I will come upon an area where a lot of the tugboats cluster. There I will find my ticket south. I need to find a particular boat that has a bright green smokestack. Then I need to hang around and try to get the captain's eye and get invited aboard. Tib adds, "Now jus cuz you be on dat boat, member de one wit de green smoke stack, dat don't mean you home free. Not everyone on dat boat is a fan of us cats like de captain. Dare might be two or tree utter cats on dat boat too. You best avoid de captain's crew."

The other wise cats of Lucky's gang all give me added tips on finding food, looking for shelter. Lucky tends to remain silent during these gatherings of the minds. One evening I find Lucky off to the other side of the barn, snuggled up in some old horse blankets. I sit down next to him then lay to rest my head. I look at my new friend. He eyes me quietly. Something is up, I thought. So I ask him,

"Lucky, you okay?" He raises his head and says he's fine. I say, "It really seems something is pestering you. Is there something you want to say to me?"

He remains silent for a few moments then looks at me. He says quietly, "You know, Axel, I think you're a great cat. My friends have really taken you in like a son. I guess I am just worried you might be taking on something that is too big for you or any cat."

I sit and think about what he said. He is right; this journey is asking a whole lot. The distance to travel, the weather, everything is lined up to keep me from making it. I understand what he is saying. Why chance such a trip? I should just stay and live a good life here because it is a good life here. But here is not where Julie is. I look and him and smile, "Yes, I know, but I have no choice. I have to get back to my Julie."

He looks at me as if he wants to add something. Then he shakes his head and says, "Well Axel, if there is any cat that can do it, I know it's you. We will all be rooting for you to make it." At that he lays his head down and closes his eyes to sleep. I feel very fortunate that I met this cat. I say good night to him and move to leave him alone.

On the eighth day, the weather warms up, and we all know it is time for me to move on. I say goodbye to everyone and lastly to Lucky. He seems sad to see me go. I tell him thanks for saving my life, and I will always remember him. We sit and stare at one another a few minutes, and then I get up and head outside. I look back, and the gang is all sitting at the edge of the barn, waving bye to me. I look at Lucky, and he perks up his head and smiles. When I turn to move on, I hear him yell, "Name one of your kits after me when y'all start having kittens, okay?"

I look back and yell "I'll name one after all of you. Good bye."

It takes several hours to get to the river using the "shortcut." I think about how that shortcut cost me over a week, but then how that shortcut also saved me from almost assuredly freezing to death. My new friends saved me and taught me so much. I hope I can use their knowledge to make my way back to Julie.

It takes me three weeks to travel the 13 or 14 bends in the river before I come upon the city of Memphis my friends told me about. I was hoping for 13 bends to get there, but it was 14. The last bend was several days by itself. Finally, there is the city just like the guys described it to me. It seems a major part of the city is across the river. This side doesn't have all the tall buildings like the other. I work my way south along the river and come upon a grouping of many boats and ships. It is late in the day by then. I spend that night sleeping for a change, rather than traveling.

The next day is a very cold day. I see that daytime is really not the best time for me to move around this area. It is full of humans coming and going from ship to ship. I elect to patiently wait till nightfall before searching out my particular tugboat. Under a full moon, I spend the whole night going from pier to pier trying to find my ride. No luck. I am somewhat discouraged, but I remember Tib telling me that it could be very possible that the boat won't be there. I might have to wait around for it. It looks like he is right. I move down river from the piers and try to find a good shelter that will allow me to watch the ships come and go.

Come and go, come and go. For three weeks, three miserable weeks, I wait. Tib's words keep me from giving up hope, but I reflect on how much closer I would be if I had continued down the river. I have now spent the last six weeks of my journey, one with Lucky and Tib and now three here, not moving, not going anywhere. But then Tib did say that it would still take me, at best, two and a half years to get back to the "Red Stick." Part of me says to start moving along, the stubborn part says sit tight.

That night, a very dark and cloudy night, I barely see a ship go by me and northward in the harbor area of ships. I cannot see the color of the smoke stack for the combination of darkness and fog. I tell myself to forget about it. It is unlikely that this one ship out of the hundreds that pass each day will be the one. But what if it is? So I trek north and search for the new arrival. From behind a group of lined up tugboats and their smoke stacks, I see something greenish swaying in and out of the stacks in the distance. I strain to see in the darkness. I move down closer, and there she is. The smoke stack is bright green just like Tib described it.

I look and listen for activity onboard, but I don't pick up anything. From behind me, I hear people enjoying their beer and food from a tavern nearby, a tavern I frequent many nights scavenging for food.

I move closer and closer to the boat. As I peer across the ship, a voice calls out "Yep, this is the boat for traveling cats." This gives me a bit of a start, then I see where the voice is coming from. There, on the deck of the boat, is another fellow cat, a freckled gray cat about my age.

"Hi, I'm Axel," I say to my fellow cat.

"I'm Gumbo," he replies. Gumbo, that's a special dish the masters love to eat back home, I remember.

"Is this the boat that the captain lets us cats hitch rides?" I ask.

"Yep, but you must get permission. Don't try to board without his knowledge. He doesn't like free loaders or unfriendlies" he says. This worries me. Gumbo sees the worried look and says, "Oh, don't worry. Just hang out, and when he comes, if he sees you, you just about got it made to be invited." I thank him and retreat to a spot not far away and wait for the captain to show.

Seems this captain is due for a break because it is ten days before he shows. In the meantime, I spend the dark hours with Gumbo each night, talking about his travels. When I grow weary of waiting, he says not to worry, that this happens many a time. I ask him how long he has been on the boat, and he says he can't remember, but it has been many a year. I ask him if he remembers Tib.

"Tib? One-eye Tib? Why yes, I remember that cat. You know him?" he asks.

I told him of our week together up north of here, fourteen not thirteen bends of the river north. He seems genuinely pleased to hear that Tib is doing fine. "That is one great cat, even if he talks funny" he says with a smile. We both laugh.

"Dat he iz," I say in the best Cajun accent I can muster.

I tell him that the place I am trying to get to is the same town where Tib got on board this ship. Gumbo then says something that does not help my anxiousness of my slow progress so far. He says that the captain doesn't always go that far south. He describes how the tugboat mostly heads south from here, but not always. Sometimes he heads north. Sometimes it heads south for just a few days, then turns around and comes back. I ask the last time it went as far as Baton Rouge. He thinks about it for a moment. I dread hearing what he is about to say. What if he says not since Tib? Gumbo then says, "Oh, I guess no more than a month ago. It goes there at least two or more times a year."

Though that is not the best news, it is promising. It really looks like I am in for several months of travelling before getting back to Julie. That is not a pleasant thought. As I am about to return to my hiding and waiting spot, I hear a voice booming from down the pier. I look at where the sound is coming from then look at Gumbo, wondering who that loud man is. Gumbo smiles and says, "It's him. Put on your best 'take me mister' face."

16

You can hear the booming voice well before you can see him, barking orders to and fro to the other humans around. I jump atop one of the pier pilings near where the tug is tied up. I figure the captain can't help but see me here. As he gets closer, I can see he is a big man, big around the middle, full grey beard, a thick neck. I sit and give my best "no big deal" look. He comes and walks by me without even a glance. Oh no, I think, I have to get on that boat. I stand and turn to look to find him standing with his hands on his hips staring at me. He smiles. Time to turn on the charm.

I stand and arch my back in a stretch and look at him. I then hop down and slowly work my way to him. I get within a few feet of him then sit and look up into his face. He smiles, showing big yellow stained teeth. He says, "And what might your name be?" At that, I stand and walk over and rub up against his rubber boots that stink of fish and oil. He looks around as if to see if I belong to anyone around here. He shrugs his shoulders and says, "Come on kitty; want to go for a ride?" Thank heavens, I thought!

I jump up on the tugboat bow and work my way over to where Gumbo is. The captain says "This here is Gumbo. He's been with me; hmmm...... he rubs his scruffy beard, then says ....going on five years now. He's the boss now, so you'd better listen or it's off the boat for you." At that, the captain, moves on inside the boat. He starts up the motor which seems very loud and constant. It seems the whole boat vibrates from the motor. Over the next several hours, several men plus the captain are on and off the boat preparing for its departure. A departure southward I pray.

It grows dark, and the captain and his men leave for the night. Gumbo says they will be back before sunlight to ship out. Where, he doesn't know. Sure enough, well before the sun comes up in the east, all the men come back. The lines are untied and soon the tugboat is drifting backwards towards the river. I close my eyes and hope we head down river and not up river. At first, we do head north which really brought me down, but Gumbo assures me that we could be just picking up something from the big city. Lucky for me, that is it. Though it seems like eternity and another lost day, later in the day, we head south.

I thought it was cold this last month waiting for the boat to show, but now it's really cold. Being on the river is cold. Gumbo laughs at me as I shiver. There's nothing like this cold he says. He is right. It seems to go right through my fur. The food is good. We get to eat the leftovers the crew doesn't save. As we travel, we stop at other ports along the way, sometimes two or three times a day. Normally around dark, we anchor and the crew sleeps.

This goes on for weeks! The weather is getting somewhat warmer. Spring must be here. Each day we travel south, I look for the bridges and the tall pointed building. Bridges come and go, but no tall pointed buildings.

I ask Gumbo if he thinks we're getting close, and he thinks about it for a while before answering. "Yes, and no" he says. He went on about how it is very possible at any of the next stops, the captain will change course back North, almost assuredly after docking for a night. He says that it is getting time for me to choose.

"Choose what" I ask?

"Choose whether to stay and gamble we still go south or will we turn north" he replies. I must have given a look of confusion so he adds, "What I'm saying to you friend, is that we are close enough, I believe, that if you went on foot, you will get there within the next few months or even weeks. If you stay, we might be there next week or even days. The problem is that we don't know. The captain may turn about at any of the next stops. One thing is for sure. He will turn eventually, but will it be before, at or even after Baton Rouge."

This is a dreadful thought. I cannot bear to be this close, then be trapped heading north again. Gumbo also says that the trip north doesn't have as many stops, so it could be quite a while before I am able to get off again. What to do, I wonder for the rest of that day. I ask Gumbo to give me his best estimate of how close we are right then. He thinks for a long while then says, "I'm thinking we are pretty close, like within a few days if we keep moving. That would be about two or three weeks by foot, I guess." I weigh my options and decide that I am basically about a year and half ahead of schedule, based on Tib's estimate. I am going to go by land at our next stop.

17

Our next stop is late that evening. I ask Gumbo what he thinks I should do, and he refuses to answer. He shakes his head and says "No, I can't do that. I would feel terrible about you staying, then the boat heads back up river. I also would feel terrible if you got off, and we headed down river and arrived later that day. No, I don't know what to tell you to do." I nod my head in understanding. I look out on the pier and gaze back to the land, then southward. "You're going, aren't you," he asks quietly. I nod. He seems very disappointed. I don't like the idea of leaving my new friend either. He looks south then says, "You're going to make it, Axel. You're almost there."

I ponder whether to let the captain see me go or not. I decide to let the men leave for the night then go. I look at Gumbo's eyes and smile; I am going to miss him. "Goodbye friend; I owe you buddy," I say and walk down the plank to the pier. He yells back to me "I'll tell Tib you made it if I see him again." I smile, then scamper down the pier toward land.

Land, the first time I have set foot on solid ground in what seems months. I travel as far as I can that first night and realize that I have gotten out of shape from the luxury of the boat. I quit for the night well before daybreak. As I travel, I keep an eye out for the tugboat. How disappointed I would be if I saw it moving down river and passing me by. Fortunately, I never see the boat again. Whether it headed north or passed me without my knowing, I don't know.

Each day I hope to see familiar landmarks. Each day I don't. After a week, I feel really down and tired. I force myself to think of Julie and how I have to get back to her. I think about Tommy and Plato, my best friend and my mentor. That always seems to put a little more hitch in my giddy-up. The weather is warmer now. All the trees are blooming fresh leaves. Some days I eat well, some days I starve, but no matter, I move on.

It is early on the tenth day after living on the boat that I spy a bridge in the distance. Just another bridge I figure. I have seen a dozen or so since my travels, but something feels different about this one. Instead of resting, I decide to continue. Around mid-day, my heart jumps when I see a second bridge further south of the bridge I spied earlier. Normally I stay away from the levee, but I need to get a better look. I run up the levee and look down river.

My heart leaps when I see the tall pointed building just south of the first bridge. Yes, that is the building close to Julie's house. Then my heart sinks, when I see that the building is on the other side of the river. What has been nagging me all my travels finally hits me. I am on the wrong side of the river. I feel like an idiot for not planning for that all along. The river has to be a mile wide here. How can I get across? The bridge is an obvious option, but there is so much traffic on a bridge. That problem occupies my brain the rest of the day. I get to the first bridge at nightfall.

18

This first bridge is a long bridge. The ramps the cars and trucks take to go over the bridge start very far away from the river. I work my way to the entrance-way of the bridge. It seems all the while travelling by foot, I rarely had to cross a road or street. When I did, it was usually just a narrow two-lane road. Here, I am surrounded by wide highways with traffic that never stops. I suddenly feel dead tired. I retreat to a nearby building and find shelter under an old abandoned truck.

What to do, I think to myself. If I can use the bridge, I can get across in twenty minutes or so. But the traffic is so horrible. I will have to walk the narrow curb alongside passing vehicles and the railing. Slipping under the railing is a possibility. The passing traffic, especially the large trucks, could sweep me under the railing, or worse, suck me into the traffic. Are there any other options? A boat...but there is no guarantee they will cross the river. I lay under that old truck throughout most of the night trying to figure out what to do. As the night passes, I notice the traffic slows, not nearly as many vehicles coming and going.

That's it. My only chance is to pick the right time when traffic is at its least and go for it. I am so close to being home that it is making my decision to watch the traffic pattern for a few days hard to accept. I have to be right on the timing or I won't get halfway, much less all the way across. I sleep and forage for food during the next few days. At night I watch the traffic. It seems that about three hours before daybreak, the traffic lessens to just a few vehicles every few minutes. That is good. What is bad is that most of the time, the vehicles are the huge trucks with the long trailers.

The next night, I decide to test myself. I try running up the beginning of the bridge for just a little ways, not too far where I can't jump down from it and land safely. I project from the traffic the start my dash and take off. I was unprepared for the steepness of the bridge. I tire badly after just a hundred feet. Then I hear it. It is one of the big trucks coming. I stop and press up against one of the railing posts, waiting for it to pass. I look down and see how I can easily slip through and off the bridge. The truck nears and the sound is deafening. As it passes, it sweeps up small rocks and sand and throws it against me. Then the wind of the passing trailer buffets me almost off my feet. I struggle to hold tight against the railing post. Wow, I thought, and that is only after just a hundred feet of bridge. The bridge is at least a mile long, so I have to cross a half-mile up and half-mile down to make it to the other side.

I go back to my resting spot under the truck and try to make sense of it all. Can I make it across without getting killed, I wondered? My initial thought is no, but then I think of Julie, so close now. I then decide tomorrow night is the time I will go for it.

It rains all the next day. This adds the wetness of the bridge into consideration. It will not just be rocks and sand blowing against me now; it will be rain and puddles of water. I could surely slip off the bridge if I go now. As much as I hate to wait, I opt to wait till the rain stops. It is two more days and nights before the time is right.

19

The time comes to say good-bye to my old truck shelter and hello to the other side of the river. The rainy weather has stopped and the roads are dry by late that afternoon. I wait all night for the time I estimate the traffic will be at its least. I know my window is short. Each minute closer to daylight, more and more traffic comes. When I finally decide it's time, I hear one of the big trucks off in the distance. I decide to wait for it to pass. I'm glad I do. It is a long line of trucks, at least ten of them all passing at once. When the last one speeds past, I take off.

Up and up the narrow curb I race as hard as I can. About halfway up, I hear a smaller vehicle coming up behind me. I debate whether to keep running or stop. I stop and let it pass. The wind buffets me, but I am ready for it. I continue running up and up. My lungs burn, as it seems forever I am running uphill. Then the hill flattens a bit, then becomes very flat. It seems the bridge is level as it crosses the river. I look down and shiver at the thought of falling that far. A row of barges are going under me, and they look like little boxes. On the flat part of the bridge, I slow to catch my breath. A few more of the smaller vehicles pass. As the bridge starts to slope downward, I can see I am getting close to the other side. I run as fast as I can.

I hear it when I am halfway down the other side. I quickly look back and cannot see it yet. I look down and see I am no longer over the river, but am far above land. The sound is loud, and I know I am in trouble. I race down the bridge. The sound grows suddenly louder, and the big truck starts down the bridge. The lights blind me when I peek back to see. I cannot see anything. I slow and try to see how close I am to the bottom. I can't see clearly. I know my only chance is to keep running down. I can barely see the railing to my right as I run. I keep it to my right shoulder as best I can. The sound is deafening as the truck approaches. I dare not look back, look down or slow down. The truck flies by me. I brace myself for the spray of rocks and sand. The wind hits me like a bat, knocking me off my feet. I feel myself slip through the opening and fall downward.

Oh no, I thought. This is it. But an instance later, I fall into the tall grass of a sloping hill and roll to the bottom. I try to cleanse my eyes with my paws. When I finally can see, I see the bridge is no more than just a few feet from the embankment I fell on. I slowly get up and circle around to check if I am okay. I am it seems. Then it hits me. I am over the bridge. I am on Julie's side of the river. My heart leaps, and I start to work my way back to the river to follow it southward.

20

When I get to the river, I climb the levee and looked south. There is the tall pointed building right in the middle of Red Stick. I look up at the bridge towering over me and the traffic as it passes. I look back over the river and can't believe I made it. I then feel the aches in my legs from the run. I realize how tired and hungry I am, but there is no stopping me now.

It takes most of the day, the longest day I can remember since I first was whisked away. I ponder the time and estimate that it has been almost a year since I last saw Julie. I smile at the thought of seeing her again in just a few hours. When I get closer to the tall pointed building, I have to guess at the point where I need to leave the river and head east towards the old house. Based on what I can remember, the building is to the west of where we lived. So I continue till the building is directly to my left from the river.

I take a long last look at the river. I look north to the bridge I crossed in the night. Beyond, I can see the river turn into one of its hundreds of bends. I see the ships, some small, some much bigger than I had seen up north, moving up and down the river. I know right then, I never want to see that river again. I shake my head and laugh and walk up and over the levee for the last time.

It being a big city, I again have to cross numerous busy streets. I eventually pass the tall building and come upon a neighborhood of familiar houses. I am here. Though I am dead tired with my muscles aching from the run across the river, and am starving, I move on. I soon come upon the street that I and my master travelled so many times to and from our house.

21

The sight of the old house makes me quiver. I am so nervous. I run down the driveway and see a strange vehicle there. Another human has moved in I see. No matter, I just want to pass through the yard. As I approach the gate, a large dog comes barking at me from inside the yard, scaring me half to death. Great, I think, travel all this way and die of a heart attack this close to Julie.

I work my way around the yard. The dog barks and follows me all the way to the back fence. I climb up the fence which makes him go even crazier. I jump down on the other side into Tommy and Julie's yard. The barking stops. Stupid dog.

I work my way through the woods to the clearing in their backyard. I can hardly wait to see her. It seems much longer than a year since I last saw her. To be able to hear her voice, to see her eyes once more brought tears to my eyes. Then I hear the boy.

"Come on Tommy, go get the toy," I hear him say. I move closer to see that the young boy is much taller now, more like a young man. I look to see a familiar Tommy rolling around on his back, but instead I see a much slimmer, muscular cat sitting atop the deck staring down at the young man. Where is Tommy, I wonder? Then I realize that I am looking at Tommy. My friend has slimmed down. In fact, he is in great shape. He's still a giant of a cat, but not fat. Way to go, my boy, I think.

The young man, Holden, finally gives up and tosses the toy away as usual. He walks up the steps and gives Tommy a gentle stroke around his neck. Tommy leans his head into him. Then I see Julie, as beautiful as ever, lying near the doorway of the house. Holden bends over and rubs her back. She stretches and smiles. Oh, what a wonderful smile. When the young man goes inside, Tommy hops down and goes over to Julie and snuggles up against her. That's my boy, watching out for Julie.

I walk a few feet into the yard then stop. I am not sure how to approach them. I sit and stare at them from afar pondering this when Tommy jumps up on the deck hand-railing. This is quite a feat for the fat cat that I had to push up the steps not long ago. He tilts his head a bit sideways looking at me. I smile. Then he knows. His eyes light up and he leaps forward to the grass and races towards me.

The force of his hit on me knocks the breath out of me. Tommy stands over me, "Axel it's you. You're back." He has tears in his eyes. I do too. I can't speak. I look towards the deck and I see Julie staring at me with a shocked look. Tommy gushes "Oh Axel, Plato told us what happened. We figured you got taken away before you could run away. Gosh I missed you; we all missed you."

I stare up into his eyes. "Will you get off me so I can breathe, big guy," I say to him. He jumps off of me. I roll over and stand up, trying to shake the stars out of my head. I mustered out "I'm back. That is all I've been trying to do for the last year is get back to my friends here." I look at Julie, and she still is sitting there in what looks like shock. "Oh Julie, I'm so sorry this happened to her. Is she okay?" I ask.

Tommy hesitates a bit then says, "Yes, Axel. She was heartbroken when you disappeared. It's been rough on her. Look, Axel...." I run towards her not letting Tommy finish. I run up the deck and wrap my paws around her and hug her tight. She hugs me back and starts crying. I start crying too. Soon Tommy is hugging us both.

22

I pull myself away from the two of them to look at Julie. She is as beautiful as ever. Tommy sits next to her, first looking at me, then away. I look at Julie, her eyes so beautiful, but filled with tears. She finally says, "Oh Axel, I'm so happy you're okay. We both missed you dearly." That is the first inkling I get that something has changed. Something is wrong. My first thought is Plato. Tell me he is alive.

"Plato! Plato is still here, right?" I beg. They look at each other a moment then back at me. Oh no, I think, my dear friend, Plato. What happened to him? My head hangs down waiting for the news.

Julie then says, "Plato missed you too."

My head perks up, "You mean he's alive." Julie nods. I say "Oh thank heavens, he's alive. I thought y'all were trying to tell me he passed away. I can't wait to see him, too." I look at them both, and there is still something not right.

I look deeply into Julie's eyes, and I see the pain of me going away, but I also see true happiness that I am alive. I look at Tommy, and I see the same happiness, but something is nagging at him, something he does not feel good about. He looks at Julie with those same love-filled eyes. Julie looks at him and nuzzles her head into his neck. She blinks out the tears in her eyes then looks at me. What I see... is that my Julie, my dear sweet Julie, is now in love with Tommy.

They see my reaction. My mouth gapes open. I back away a few inches. I try to comprehend it all. They both move towards me, but I hold up a paw. They stop. I look at them and don't want to believe what I am seeing. Julie starts to say something, but I don't hear it. I know I have to get out of there. I bound off the deck and run off around the house as fast as I can. I run through their front yard and off towards Plato's place.

23

When I get to Plato's, I don't stop. I run past his house to a group of bushes. I go in and lie down. I curl up and tell myself to go to sleep. I'll wake up from this nightmare, and it will be all over, I am thinking to myself. I squeeze my eyes closed hard and try to eliminate the sounds around me. I must have succeeded because when I wake up, I find it almost nightfall. The run across the bridge, the starving, and the exhaustion must have caught up with me. I slept the whole afternoon.

I open my eyes, but don't stir. I don't have the will to even stand up. All I can think about is my Julie, how I travelled so far, risked everything to get back to her, and now she is in love with another, my best friend Tommy. I close my eyes, wanting to go back to sleep forever, when I sense another presence. I raise my head and look around quickly. The site of Plato sitting just a few feet away startles me. The site of my old friend eases my pain. I look at him with sad eyes. I stand up, walk over and brush up against him. I can see he has tears in his eyes, too.

"Oh, Plato. You don't know how good it does me to see you" I say to him quietly. At that, he looks away from me blinking out some tears. The old cat is happy to see me also. I look at him long and hard. I can tell he feels my pain, but I don't want him fretting over me. I try to cheer him up. "Old friend, don't worry about me, okay? I will survive." He looks at me, showing me such pain. I know I have to put him at ease. I look at him, trying to make eye contact. "Plato, I'm happy for them both, really. I shouldn't have expected Julie to wait for me. Everyone thought I was gone for good."

Plato stands then moves and sits a few feet facing away from me. I wait patiently for his wise words to begin. After a few minutes I hear him say "Axel. You're like a son to me. I was heartbroken when you suddenly disappeared. I figured your plan to escape failed because your master took you by surprise. Just as you said, the big trucks showed up a day after we first noticed you were gone. I'd hoped you were in hiding. But knew since we agreed you would hide out here with me, I knew you were gone." At this, his head lowers, and I can hear sniffling.

I stand up and go sit beside him. I wait for him to continue. "Poor Tommy cried like a baby when you disappeared. He wallowed around on his back for hours. None of his girlfriends could console him. Then there's Julie. She was heartbroken. She came to see me about a week after, and I told her of your fears that you were moving and your plans of escape. I told her how you didn't want to worry her; how we both agreed it would be best to keep it from her until it was all over. I told her that the big trucks had come after you had already been taken away."

Again he has to gather himself. He continues. "She loved you more than anything, Axel. She was heartbroken. Thank goodness for Tommy. He was her rock to lean on. They both helped each other with their pain."

He then looks at me again with such sad eyes. I look at him and smile. "Its okay, Plato. I don't blame them at all. It's something I have to accept. I'll get over it, someday," I lie. I will never get over it, I think.

He looks at me and still there seems to be no relief to his pain. He sits a long while then says "About a month after you were gone, Julie came to see me. We talked about how we all missed you. She talked of how Tommy was there for her. How much Tommy loved her and that she loved Tommy. She then asked me if I thought you would ever come back."

At this, I see the true source of his pain. The wise old cat told her what she needed to hear to help her move on. I put a paw around him to quiet him down. I look at him and say, "Oh Plato. I will always love you like a father. You and I know what the chances were of my coming back. You did the right thing telling her I wasn't. Moving on was what she needed to do."   We both blink back tears.

After a moment, Plato says quietly, "I told her that Tommy was a good cat and loved her more than anyone could. I told her that there was no shame in loving him back. I told her you were not coming back, and she needed to accept that. I'm so sorry, Axel." He then leans his head into me. I fight hard to hold back my tears. The tears for my loss, for Plato's pain, for Julie's heartbreak, for Tommy's guilt. Tommy's guilt I thought. I have to see him as soon as I can.

24

I stay with Plato that night. I hang around his porch most of the morning waiting for Tommy. I know he'll come over eventually to check on his dad and to see if I am around. Sure enough, he comes walking slowly up the yard towards the old house. I decide to meet him outside. I quickly step out and walk towards him. The big cat seems almost frightened of me. I look him in the eyes and see the same kind of pain I saw in Plato's eyes. I can't keep looking into them, I think, without breaking down. "Come on," I say, "Let's go for a walk."

We walk our old route when he was the big roly-poly cat, but this time I do not have to slow down for him. He has to slow down for me in my weakened state. We walk for quite a while before we say anything. He comes to a stop and sits. He finally looks at me and says softly, "Julie was heartbroken when you disappeared, Axel. She cried for weeks on end for you. We both hoped you would somehow come back. After a while, she accepted the fact you were gone. She still cried and ached for you. Eventually the crying stopped. I worked hard to cheer her up. After some time, she started to smile again. Then one day, she told me she loved me, and that she wanted to be with me forever." He blinks out some tears. It is hard to look at this brute of a cat and see him weeping. "That was the best day of my life, Axel" he adds. "I love you, Axel, and I feel so bad for you, but I love her with all my life. So......are things going to change now?"

I look deep into his pained eyes. I know he is frightened to death. He is afraid Julie will leave him for me. I look away and wonder it myself. She was mine before, shouldn't she be mine now? But I know that is not to be. Tommy will be good for her, and she will be happy with him. I place a paw on his shoulder and say, "Friend, I love you both, but what is in the past, is in the past. I won't try to change what has happened here. I promise you that, my brother." With that, Tommy hugs me tight to the point I can't breathe. He releases me and we both smile at each other through teary eyes.

We finish our walk and Tommy goes to check on Julie. I ask him to ask her if she would come see me. He seems a bit uneasy about this request, but promises he will try.

25

I am home barely a full day and my whole world is turned upside down. Late that afternoon, Julie comes to see me at Plato's place. When she comes in, Plato says hello and excuses himself. Being alone with my Julie is very difficult for me to handle. I want to rush up and hold her tight, smell her fur. Julie's eyes show redness from tears. Before she can speak a word, she breaks down in tears. I want to hold her, but I think it would be wrong. But I can't just let her sit there and cry. I walk over and sit next to her. The brush of her fur next to mine is heavenly. She leans into me and cries "I'm so sorry, Axel. I'm sorry for all of this."

I lean into her and say, "I know you are. I'm sorry, too."

I wanted to say how she was the only reason I wanted to live, how I had endured so many troubles on my journey back, how she kept me alive. Instead I say. "It's okay, Julie, I'm truly happy for you, for you both."

She looks into my eyes. I did my best to convince her it is the truth. It's sort of truth, I guess. She smiles her incredible smile back at me. "Thank you, Axel. Tommy and I will always be your friends, you know that," she says sadly.

I know that, but can I handle it? Can I continue to stick around and see the cat I love be loved by my best friend and she love him back? I can't see it. I think.... there's Gumbo and the tugboat. And what about Lucky and Tib up north? Maybe I need to leave and start a new life so I don't disrupt theirs. Finally, after several minutes, I decide I will stay and give it a try and see how it goes, but I honestly feel I need to leave.

26

I spend the next several weeks living with Plato. He seems to enjoy my company, but I sense he still feels guilty about what has happened. Tommy and I take our usual walks, but I feel a difference in our friendship, too. I'm sure he still feels guilty about Julie and maybe even somewhat threatened by me. My presence here is the only thing that can cause a problem with him and Julie, and he is probably right. Julie and I chat. She seems to accept the fact that I have moved on, even tries to set me up with a few of the neighborhood girlfriends.

I act well I believe. On the outside, I seem to have accepted it all and moved on, but on the inside, I still ache to be with Julie. I hurt every time she laughs with Tommy or nuzzles with him. Only Plato can see through me; I beg him not to let my secret out. After a while, all seemed fine in our world here, but it was short-lived.

Part III

1

My poor Julie, just when I think she is going to be happy for the rest of her life with Tommy, she comes to me with terrible news. She asks Plato if she can speak to me alone. She is very agitated and upset. I sit and watch her walk back and forth. I want to hold her more than anything, but know I can't. She finally stops and comes to sit directly in front of me. Her eyes show something is terribly wrong.

"I have to talk to you, Axel. It's hard to get away without Tommy knowing. Something bad is about to happen," she says. Now that gets my full attention.

"What? What is it?" I ask.

She struggles to tell me. Finally she says "I'm pretty sure the boy of the house, Holden," she looks at me, and I nod my understanding, "is going off to college soon, moving out," she says. That doesn't seem so bad to me. Tommy can now quit with the shenanigans with the red toy. "No, you don't understand, he will be taking Tommy with him." she says as she collapses into my paws.

Now that is bad news, or is it? Tommy leaving means I will lose my best friend, but it could also mean that Julie and I can be together again. I shake the selfish thought out of my head immediately. I ask her how she knows. She tells me she heard Holden talking about his new apartment far away somewhere. His parents argue with him about taking Tommy. They want Tommy stay here with her, and that she would be heartbroken without Tommy. The son refuses and saying he is taking Tommy with him.

"When?" I ask. She shook her head, "I'm not sure, but I think they were talking about a week or so. It's hard to tell."

"Does Tommy know?"

"Gosh no, he never listens to the masters. You know that."

I laugh at that, and she tried to also.

"Oh, Axel. I will surely die of heartbreak if he leaves," she says gravely. It stings my heart to hear that. Not so much her heartache, but my heartache. Then she adds "But it's not me I'm worried about. You and I know how much he cares for me. If he's taken away, and we are separated, he will surely die." She is right. If any one of us could die of heartbreak, it would be the big brute. Losing Julie will kill him.

"What are we going to do?" she cries. A strange question, I think. We? Again, the selfish side of me is irritated by this, but I push it away. I say, "We'll think of something. Meanwhile don't tell Tommy. Let's not get him all fearful about everything." She nods her head in agreement. She gives me a short, ever-so-short, hug and then leaves.

A few moments later Plato comes inside. I explain the situation to him. He looks grim about it all, and is worried sick for his boy and for Julie. I ask if he has any ideas. He muses for a while then says quietly, "Somehow we have to convince that kid to leave Tommy or replace him with someone else," he says gently. I look at him trying to figure what he means by someone else. He looks away. I sit awhile pondering what he was saying then I walk outside. I look over the front yard trying to think of how to save Tommy and Julie. It comes to me in a flash and I realize what Plato has implying. I jump and head towards Tommy's house. The plan has to start now.

2

I hang out at Tommy and Julie's house the rest of the day. Meanwhile, the young man comes home in his little pickup truck. He goes inside, carrying a packet of those familiar cardboard boxes. He is going to be packing, I'm afraid. The time is even shorter than we thought.

I wait the rest of afternoon in their backyard, hoping Holden will come out. Later that evening, Holden does come outside. I spy the red toy in the yard and charge after it. As he looks on, I jump on the toy and wrestle with it. I grab it with my mouth and shake it vigorously. Then I freeze as if I have just seen the boy. Holden chuckles at me. I then trot towards him with the toy still in my mouth. I drop it at his feet then rub against his legs with my body. "Well I'll be," I hear him say. He then picks up the toy and tosses it. I run after it and tackle it again.

I look at him and he motions with his hand to bring it to him. I grab the toy with my mouth and bring it to him, again dropping it and rubbing up against him. Holden laughs aloud then looks around for something or someone. "You see, Tommy boy, see how it's done. Your friend here, Axel, knows how to..." he stops short. He seems a bit confused all of sudden. He eyes me strangely. "Hey, I thought you moved away with that pretty woman over there," he said pointing in the direction of my old house. "How did you get back here?"

He kneels down and pets me. I sit down and look up into his eyes. This boy Holded seems to have a kind face. He looks intently into my eyes, then says "It is you? Axel right? How did you get back here?" He stands and looks towards the old house. He knows that someone else lives there now and they have a very loud dog. He looks down at me. "You came back to be with your friends, huh?" he asks. I stand and rub up against his leg with my body.

He turns and goes back into the house. I run to the back of the yard into the woods to gather myself. Those last few moments sent gave me the willies which took a few minutes to get off me. I hate acting like a dog. But I know it just might work.

3

The next day I join both Tommy and Julie sunning ourselves on the backyard deck. We say very little. Around mid afternoon, as every afternoon, the boy Holden comes outside. "Come on Tommy," he says as he steps down into the yard. Tommy gets up and rolls his eyes at me and follows him out into the yard. The young man picks up the toy and shows it to Tommy, then tosses it out into the yard. Tommy lies down and rolls over on his back. I spring into action at that moment. I scamper across the deck and leap into the yard to chase down the toy. I attack it with vigor then bring it back to the young man. I drop it at his feet. He stoops over, picks it up then looks disgustedly at Tommy, "You see there boy, that is how you do it." Then he tosses it again across the yard, but further.

I run after it, playing the fool, and bring it to him. I notice that Tommy is eyeing me curiously as if I am crazy. Julie is now sitting on the edge of the deck watching me through confused eyes. Her head tilted in bewilderment. They both think I've gone bonkers. Holden picks up the toy and throws it even further into the yard. I run and get it and trot it back to him. I drop it at his feet and then rub up against his legs. He smiles and kneels down to pet me. He then picks me up and rubs my neck. I have to admit, this does feel good. I push my head and neck up against his hand not wanting him to stop. He walks on up the deck and places me down next to Julie. He taps my head and says as he goes into the house "Good cat, good cat."

I try to ignore Julie's incredulous look but finally I look at her. She has this "Have you gone bonkers look?" in her eyes. Tommy ambles over and sits on the opposite side of me staring at me too. I look at him and he still is eyeing me strangely. I then say, "What?" to him. He chuckles and says, "If I didn't know you better, I could swear you're trying to take my place as my master's pet." He shakes his head and moves off to lie down. I can't look at Julie. I can feel her eyeing me, but I just can't look at her right now. I step down in the grass to leave and say, "Gotta go, going to see what Plato is up to." I run off around the corner, keeping my eyes away from Julie's.

4

That night I can't sleep. I roll fitfully around. I can hear Plato snoring quietly, resting peacefully. I need to go for a walk. I step outside and it is a cool, clear night; the moon is full. I walk around the old house to take a sip of water. Why I did it, I still don't know to this day, but I decide to go to our old meeting place, the place where Julie and I had our late evening dates when everyone else was asleep.

I get there and feel I should leave right away, but I don't. I climb up the fence and sit down on the post where Julie and I would sit together. I look up at the moon, and it seems so much bigger in the sky. I think back to how perfect life was just a year ago. No matter how I seem to the others, I still miss being with Julie. There will never be another cat like her in my life. I suddenly feel really tired; I am ready to go to sleep.

I lower myself to the ground and am nearly startled out of my skin to see Julie sitting just a few feet away. "I will always cherish those nights we spent here, Axel," she says quietly. Me, too, I say to myself. I don't feel comfortable being here alone with Julie. I don't trust myself alone with her. I imagine grabbing her and hugging her close to me. I want to dearly. I steel myself, smile at her, and continue to walk back towards the old house. I don't have the courage to say anything without choking up. I manage a pretty fair, "Good night, Julie."

She comes up alongside me and tries to look me in the eyes. I again cannot. I walk on looking around everywhere but at her. I can tell she wants to thank me for what I am trying to do. When Tommy said that I was trying to replace him, I knew Julie saw through me then. Now she's trying to thank me for doing something that she knows in her heart is very hard for me to do. She knows the only happy outcome for her and Tommy, if this works, is for me to go away with Tommy's master, to replace him like Tommy said. My pace quickens. I know she is grateful, but it doesn't make me feel better. Not right here next to her.

As I close in on the old house, she swats at me, actually drawing a bit of blood, I think. I yelp and wonder what the heck she's doing. Her eyes tell me to stop trying to run from this. I relent and sit down and look into her wonderful eyes once again. She looks back at me, and I think I will melt right there. Then she says softly "Axel, thank you for trying to help Tommy. It tears me apart thinking I have to lose either of you. It all seems so unfair to you, Axel." She looks away. Now she can't look at me. I wait for her to look back at me. When our eyes meet again, I say "I'm not doing this for Tommy, my dear Julie. I'm doing this for you." I can see tears forming in her eyes as well as feel them in mine. "I love you more than anything and I want you to be happy. Yes, it does seem unfair, but it's the right thing to do --the only thing to do." With that, I say good-night to her with my eyes and walk back into Plato's lair.

I listen and eventually I hear my Julie walking her way back home. I watch her through the openings of the porch walking slowly then trotting out of sight. I suddenly feel so tired. I practically fall over on my side and curl up to try to sleep. I feel so lonely. I hear a sniffle from Plato's way. I look, and he is awake in the darkness looking at me. His eyes show great kindness and love. I smile weakly back at him. If all goes according to plan, I will be losing my old friend here, too.

5

The next day I wake with a start. Julie is shaking me awake. "Axel, wake up. It's too late. The Holden boy is packing up his truck right now. He's getting ready to leave." She is in tears. I jump up and try to think of what to do. I tell her to run home and stay with Tommy. No matter what, stay close to him. You have got to show your masters that Tommy has to stay. "Go now!" She hesitates then runs off.

Plato seems to stir, but is slow to fully awaken. This could be the last time I see him, I thought. I run over to him and hug him tightly. "Good-bye friend. I love you," I say, running off before I start to cry. I run over as fast as I can. When I get there, the Holden boy is putting something into the back of his truck which seems to be loaded up with boxes and furniture. I hear his mother saying something about please leave him here. I look through the window and see Tommy and Julie watching the boy load up his truck. They are sitting closely together. The boy's mother then points to the cats in the window and says something like, "Look Holden, see how much they care for each other." With perfect timing, Julie nuzzles her head into Tommy's neck. Tommy leans his head into hers. Way to go girl I thought.

I had to act now. I run around the truck and into the backyard to get the toy. I can't find it. Oh no, I thought, maybe he has put it away. I was hoping to use it as a last ditch effort on the boy. Then I spy it on the deck. I run up, grab it and run to the front. The boy is adjusting some of the boxes in the back of the truck with his father. I move in closer and bite harder into the toy, making it squeak. Holden turns and looks down to see me sitting and looking up at him. He smiles and takes the red toy out of my mouth saying, "Thanks, Axel, I almost forgot this; Tommy is going to need it."

I look up at the window to see if Tommy hears what the boy said. He is looking away at something else. Thank goodness, I say to myself. I stand and rub up against the boy's legs. The mother then asks "Is that Axel? I thought he had moved away." He then stoops over, picks me up and rubs my neck. I close my eyes and push up against the rubbing fingers. I force myself to purr. Despite all the acting I'm doing, I do really like this part.

"Yes, can you believe it, he says. I think he found his way back to be with our cats again. I think he's living outside. I don't know where he's...where he's...living." The boy seems to hesitate a bit at the last statement. I close my eyes tight, hoping with all my might that the plan is working.

"Well, he seems attached to you, son, and he likes that stupid toy you've been trying to teach Tommy to fetch. Wouldn't it make more sense to take him instead of splitting Tommy and Julie apart?" his mother implores. With that, I see a look of fear come into Tommy's eyes. Julie tries to calm him by nuzzling closer to him.

The Holden boy looks at me, then at his cat in the window. He smiles and shakes his head. "You're right, mom. All along y'all have been trying to tell me to leave Tommy here, and here is a cat ready to go with me." He looks at me and says, "You want to go on a trip, boy?" I close my eyes, trying to keep from looking at my friends, and push my head into his chest.

It happens fast after that. I find myself inside the cab of the truck. The parents hug their boy good-bye. I stand up and try to see past them into the window, but I can't see Tommy and Julie. The boy then climbs in and starts up the truck. As we start moving down the driveway, I catch a glimpse, just a glimpse, of them before we turn out of the driveway. Through my keen eyes, I see Julie's eyes; they were grateful. I see my buddy, Tommy, holding up a paw, waving good-bye. I am ready to sink down in the seat when I realize we will be passing by Plato's house. I strain to see him, and don't think I will and then I see him on the sidewalk. He is saluting me; I salute back.

I feel good that the plan worked, but it is still so sad for me. It seems everything worked out for everyone except for me. The Holden boy then says something that wakes me out of my stupor. He reaches over and pulls me up, rubs his face up against me and says, "You're going to like my new place, Axel. Not much yard, but there's a pool. Oh, and the neighbor next to me has two cats. You like Siamese cats?"

"Say What!"

Epilogue

Life with Holden, my new master has been grand. The new place is great and it appears that my master has quite a way with the female humans. Seems many come by to visit and just love to hold and pet me, which I really don't mind. And true to his word, I am realizing my dream of Siamese cats. Both are beautiful females, and both cannot get enough of me. We spend just about all our free time, when we're not with our masters, together.

I often think about my friends, Tommy, Julie and Plato. Unbeknownst to all of us is the fact that my master did not move that far away and often goes home on weekends. Most of the time he takes me along so I still get to see my friends. It is always a big reunion when we get together.

On one of the visits back home, Tommy got me alone and gave me a long, huge hug. He looked at me, but said nothing. I didn't say anything either. We both said it all with our eyes. About a year later, my master and I went home to a house full of kittens. Some looked like Tommy, some looked like Julie. "Uncle Axel," I hear as I entered the house and am mobbed by a half-dozen kittens.

My last visit though, was a sad one and the reason I decided to tell this story. My dear friend Plato passed away in his sleep. Gone to cat heaven I'm sure. I spent a long time lying down and weeping on his grave behind the old house. A really strange thing happened, too. After lying there and finally gathering all my wits, I stood up to said good-bye and leave. A strange but familiar voice came from just a few feet behind me, "I must admit he was a good, wise and kind cat."

I looked to see a much older Spite sitting there. For a moment I sense danger, but one look in his eyes, I saw that a change had come over him. I learn that after our "party," he left his gang and wandered around much of the city. He ended up living by the river where he met another cat, an old wise one-eyed cat named Tib. My jaw must have dropped because Spite noticed it. He asked if I knew him, and I said I had met him further up river. I relay the story of how I had worked my way down the river to get back here. He shook his head and smiled, "Small world we live in, huh, son?" He then told of how Tib had convinced him to change his wicked ways. He then said he heard about Plato's passing and wanted to come pay his respects. We tapped paws, parted ways and I never saw him again.

Finally, I do want to clarify why I stepped in and took Tommy's place as my new master's pet. Julie was right about

Tommy. He would have died from heartbreak being separated from her. I know that for sure. I'm glad it worked out for him and I'm truly happy for him. I also sort of fibbed to Julie when I said I was doing it for her too. True I did want her to be happy. If not with me then with my best friend, the new love in her life. If I could keep them together, I knew they would live a long and happy life.

But that is not why I did what I did. I did it for me. I had girlfriends before Julie and several since, but none stole my heart like her. Being around her after I returned, even though she was clearly happy, brought an inner ache deep inside me. Most of the time these days I truly enjoy the time with Julie, Tommy and their kittens. But, it is when I am alone when that the memory of my love for Julie always creeps into my heart. It is even worse when we are alone together, even if just for a brief moment. I'll never lose that incredible urge to want to sweep her up and hold her tight against me. Knowing then that I would have to leave or keep this heartache inside me until it killed me, the opportunity to kill two birds with one stone came along. I could save Tommy, and I could keep Julie happy. But it was the opportunity for me to leave and for them to not feel guilty about me leaving. If I had moved on alone, they would have both known why, and I did not want that pain or guilt on them. No, this move was to save my life.

So that's my story. Hope it didn't make you as sleepy as I am right now. I'm sitting here with this huge dilemma now. Do I go visit my Siamese girls or take a nap? What would Plato do, I wonder? That's an easy one.

Nap, it is.

The End

Printed in Great Britain
by Amazon